George C. Booth

THE FOOD AND DRINK OF MEXICO

Illustrated by
Cas Duchow

Dover Publications, Inc., New York

TO MY WIFE, SUSIE BOOTH

Published in Canada by General Publishing Com-
pany, Ltd., 30 Lesmill Road, Don Mills, Toronto,
Ontario.
Published in the United Kingdom by Constable
and Company, Ltd., 10 Orange Street, London
WC 2.

This Dover edition, first published in 1976, is an
unabridged republication of the work originally
published in 1964. It is reprinted by special arrangement with the original publisher, The Ward
Ritchie Press, 474 South Arroyo Parkway, Pasadena,
California 91105.

International Standard Book Number: 0-468-23314-6
Library of Congress Catalog Card Number: 75-39349

Manufactured in the United States of America
Dover Publications, Inc.
180 Varick Street
New York, N.Y. 10014

CONTENTS

WHEN Mulai el-Krim, the Moor, rode proudly into Spain, he sneered at the sparse foods of the infidel land. It was a dry country where Mulai saw occasional herdsmen tending scrawny cattle, pigs—which Muslims considered unclean—sheep and goats. He saw dusty vineyards and olive orchards, but he looked in vain for the watered gardens and citrus groves he had left in Morocco, and he found no sign of his cherished rice, spices and coffee.

Mulai found, however, that the Spaniard and his bony horse or mule could campaign for weeks on an occasional hatful of water and a gourd of thin wine. It was obvious that the nag could find a rare pocket of dry graze, but what fueled this fanatical Iberian who dared stand against the invincible armies of the Prophet?

As the months of bitter campaigning turned into years, Mulai learned much about his tough foe. The Spaniard turned out to be the world's master at preserving meat; he knew every trick connected with drying, salting, smoking, pickling and curing with herbs.

So, while Mulai and his squadrons held the valleys, built their palaces and irrigated newly introduced plants and trees, the Spaniard stubbornly held the dry mountains. With a few pounds of dry meat, garbanzos and a head of garlic he was self-sufficient for weeks. If he were harried he could gnaw a hard sausage or strip of dry beef on the gallop; given an hour he could roast a clove of garlic and pound it with a handful of dried beef, add a cup of wine and boil it over a quick fire in his small clay pot and drink a nourishing soup. When a group of Spanish raiders made a day's stop they pooled the meats, bones and withered vegetables from their saddle bags and cooked them in a huge clay pot which they called a *puchero*.

Today not one Mexican in ten thousand knows that a *puchero* is a cooking pot, but Mexico's most popular family feast, Spanish boiled dinner, is called *puchero*. The ingredients are still about the same as they were in the Guadarrama mountains more than a thousand years ago.

Puchero Español

1 cup garbanzos (chick peas)	Salt and pepper
1 small cured pork hock with bone	¼ tsp. ground clove
	Pinch saffron
2 slices salt pork	3 cloves garlic
2 beef soup bones	4 carrots
1 link *chorizo*—Spanish sausage	3 turnips
2 slices blood sausage —blutwurst	3 leeks
	2 onions
2 lbs. boiling beef	6 mild red chiles
½ lb. lean pork	Handful parsley
1 chicken chopped in small pieces	1 small cabbage
	6 leaves swiss chard
2 slices bacon	

Soak the garbanzos, pork hock, salt pork, soup bones and sausage overnight.

In the morning put all the meat and chicken on to cook in the water in which it soaked. When the pot has boiled as fiercely as the blood of a Spaniard for an hour, add the garbanzos and salt. Two hours later smuggle pepper, cloves, saffron and ground garlic into the *puchero*. When the meat is tender add whole peeled vegetables, remembering to seed and peel chiles also. After another hour's cooking drop in the cabbage and chard, simmer 40 minutes more, and the *puchero* is ready for a cavalier's undivided attention. Serve the drained garbanzos on one platter with the vegetables around them. The sliced meat and chicken is dispensed from a second platter and the strained *caldo*, or soup, is proudly ladled from a tureen. Serves eight liberally.

The Spaniard gained so much heart from his clay pot that he gradually hounded the invader from his land. As Mulai's descendants slunk out of Spain, twenty-eight generations after their arrival, they paused in a high pass for a last look at the land they had remade. A vast irrigation system led water for miles to nourish oranges, lemons and tangerines—the orange of Tangiers.

Dozens of fruits, vegetables and cereals were now as much a part of Spain's permanent booty as the palatial Alhambra. Mulai the twenty-ninth could take whatever bitter pleasure he wished from the fact that his countrymen had marked the Spanish language with the names of their foods, and that provisions which had been luxuries to the hungry Spaniard when he had first plundered Moorish supply trains were now integrated into his ordinary diet. Later the Spaniard would introduce these foods to the rest of Europe and to the Americas which he would discover this very year.

Many of Mulai's descendants remained in Spain, and one of them, José Mulai López, landed at Vera Cruz, Mexico, with Cortés twenty-seven years after the Moors left Spain. José Mulai took as dim a view of the heathens he was attempting to plunder as his distant ancestor had of the Spaniards. One day José was with a raiding party which captured a large village and as part of the booty he was given a seventeen-year-old-girl named Zochee. From that day José gained a fonder feeling for the country and its people.

The Indians provisioned the Spaniards with foods they had never dreamed of, and each day Zochee turned out novel and exciting dishes. Once José brought a piece of bacon and a dry onion from the dwindling quartermaster's supplies and presented it to the girl. The next evening when he returned to camp he discovered his precious food in a bubbling clay *olla* filled with a red and brown stew.

"What's that?" José pointed to the large brown seeds.

"*Frijol*," she replied and ladled him a portion.

"What's this red stuff?" he asked suspiciously.

"*Tomatl y chile*."

He sniffed, and the aroma was heavenly, so he took a bite and found the taste even better.

"Bueno," he reported. "The sainted Lord intended my little bacon and onion to live in peace with beans and tomatoes and chile."

While the army lay near the coast, Zochee fed José such seafoods as he had never dreamed of. She wrapped fish in banana leaves and roasted them in a small pit with sweet potatoes, or gave him shrimp or oysters in a sauce of tomatoes and chile. In no time at all José came to expect a golden banana, savory papaya or juicy pineapple as the natural complement to his meal.

On her stone *metate*, Zochee constantly ground corn soaked in lime water to make a dough which she patted into tortillas or rolled around meat and seafood to make a *tamal* or *charupa*. For a breakfast beverage she dropped a ball of the dough into hot sweetened water and served him *atole*, or whipped cacao and vanilla into frothy chocolate.

During the long months of hard marching and bitter fighting that followed, Zochee tended José Mulai well. When Mexico was conquered José was granted a land holding near Cuernavaca, and he settled down with Zochee in a large house which his Indians made of their native adobe.

As soon as regular shipments were coming from Spain, José was able to stock his place with a few horses, cattle, pigs and chickens and to plant sugar cane, rice, onions and garlic along with the native plants. Zochee blended the new and old foods with an intuitive skill that turned out many a culinary triumph.

She and her daughters learned many Spanish recipes, but they never hesitated to substitute whatever they had for ingredients they lacked, and they were daring in adding favorite herbs and local vegetables.

Zochee's daring passed through the centuries to her descendants, giving them courage to blend chocolate, garlic and chile into *mole*. Thousands of others have exercised equal imagination to develop the unique, indigenous cuisine that is Mexican cookery.

MEXICANS eat three meals a day, but their timing and purpose differ from the daily three meals of the North American. "Man does not live by bread alone" could well sum up the philosophy of their eating habits.

A meal in Mexico seems to be primarily social, with alimentation taking a back seat. Constant, animated conversation continues from the moment the diners sit down until the last one rises —perhaps two or three hours later. The courses come slowly and so do the waiters, but *que le hace?*—what does it matter? The next course will arrive in due season, and in the meantime there are all those dear friends, relatives and discussions.

Unless an American eats at a tourist hotel run on American schedule he will find himself out of phase until he picks up the Mexican timing.

By the time most restaurant owners have taken down the shutters in the morning, fired up the charcoal range and leisurely sloshed down the tile floor, it is well past nine o'clock. An *Almuerzo* generally consists of orange juice, coffee or whipped chocolate, and sweet cakes. Mexicans are artists with sweet dough, and the variety of their creations is endless. The waiter brings in a platter heaped high with cookies, cake, coffee cake, claws and doughnuts—and when you have finished *almuerzo* he counts the stack and charges you for the number missing.

Should you wish to breakfast at seven or eight, then it is well to join the taxi drivers and street sweepers in the plaza where fruit juice is squeezed while you wait and itinerants hawk frozen custards, *atole, tacos* and *empanadas*.

The upper classes, however, do not get out until ten o'clock, and by eleven the open front cafes are bursting with business. Everyone has had a chance to wake up in Christian fashion, and gay groups smile and chatter as they look approvingly at ranch style eggs, omelettes, thick slices of ham and plate smothering steaks. Each dish is flanked by refried beans and straw baskets of *bolillos*, the hard Mexican roll.

At one o'clock the shutters go up over the stores and all business closes down for siesta until three or four. Now comes the nub of life for the Latin American, the two hour dinner, called the *comida*. The entire family gathers at home, and only those too far away to return to their families are found in the restaurants.

Wherever it is served, the order of the *comida* is as mandatory as a high mass. It consists of seven courses,

1. *Entremés*
2. *Sopa*
3. *Pasta* or dry soup
4. Fish
5. Fowl or meat with salad
6. *Postre* or dessert
7. Tea or coffee

An *entremés* is a canape or appetizer which may range from a cracker with mashed sardine on top to a chilled seafood cocktail. Unexpected variations in colors, components and shapes are encountered.

As I have explained at some length in the chapter on soups, the Mexicans are great soup lovers and creators; they are not as suave as the French, but they are bolder. A regular soup or broth is served for course two, then a dry soup or *pasta* follows. The *pasta* is any form of rice, macaroni, spaghetti, noodle or vermicelli, or a Spanish *budín* of meat or vegetable.

Fish is served in any form and generously, always supplemented with ample supplies of sliced lime. Meat also is provided in a wide range with constant fresh methods of dressing. Vegetables are rarely featured by themselves; they come in the soup, in the *pasta*, in the meat sauce, or flank the meat on the serving platter.

Dessert or *postre* covers a wide field. You may be flattered with candied yam, stewed fruit, the ever popular *flan* or custard, ice cream or cake. You can, however, be certain that the coffee will not be served until every crumb of your *postre* is gone. I have carried on many a well-thought-out campaign to get coffee with cake, but the waiter always circumvented me. It just isn't done; the coffee comes last and you are supposed to sip genteelly for half an hour with a cigarette or cigar to put a period to the correct meal.

Cena, or supper, is another meal that follows precedent, but it lacks the singlemindedness of *comida*. The *comida* is the day's big meal; *cena* is lighter, shorter and generally eaten more quickly. The supper has six courses:

1. *Entremés*
2. *Sopa*
3. Fish

4. Fowl or meat
5. *Postre*
6. Coffee or chocolate

Whereas in the *comida* one is likely to get a cream soup or a hearty bowl, at night a consommé is usual, and the meat is frequently cold sliced or redone in one of the many recipes for leftover meat.

If *padre* decides to take his family out for *cena*, everyone goes from the grandparents to the youngest babe. Again everything is jolly, and no one scolds or clucks impatiently at the children. The youngsters have so much fun they forget to leave anything on their plates.

Cena is also time to have a few drinks with the meal; however middle and upper class Mexicans are light drinkers and frequently make a bottle of beer or wine last until midnight. The earliest respectable time to start *cena* is eight o'clock, but the maximum groups of jovial diners crowd the cafes at ten and eleven.

The Mexican version of the coffee break is the *merienda*, a little bonus meal or lunch. Office and store workers ordinarily work from nine in the morning until one o'clock, and they like to go out in groups of no less than a dozen from ten thirty to eleven thirty and have a small steak with coffee and sweet bread. The *merienda* tides one over from a light breakfast to the two o'clock *comida*.

So, if you wish to entertain with a Mexican meal, take your choice between *almuerzo, merienda, comida* or *cena* and you have almost endless variations. *More than twenty thousand variations are possible from the recipes in this book.*

The barbecue is in a different genre. Barbecuing was developed in Texas, New Mexico, Arizona and California from the Mexican *barbacoa*, but it is completely distinct. The true border barbecue is built around one main dish—usually outdoor grilled meat with salad, garlic toasted french bread and fruit jam served with a pot of steaming coffee.

The New England clam bake, the fish fry and the Hawaiian luau have created an American institution, the cookout. Practically anything goes, and dozens of recipes in this book are admirably suited for a barbecue or cookout.

Sopas

Sopas

SOME LIKE IT HOT

THE SECOND COURSE in any well-ordered Mexican lunch or dinner is a soup which is generally as intriguing as its name. If the menu says *sopa*, your waiter may bring in a hearty soup that varies from liquid to dry; *sopa de arroz* or rice soup has all the water steamed out and is similar to our fried rice.

All broth is *caldo*, but a liquid soup with meat, vegetables or seafood is also *caldo*. Clear, strained broth is *boullon* or *consomé*, and chilled vegetable soup is *gazpacho*.

To show that he is never bound by regulations the Mexican chef may serve *sopa* as a soup course, or in the third course which is called the *pasta*. I have been served *pozole*, *puchero* and *paella* as soups, *pastas* and main dishes. Hard rolls, called *bolillos*, quartered limes and fresh *salsa* are mandatory with any soup.

The Aztecs were adding tropical fruits to their soup long before the Spaniards arrived, and they quickly learned the old Moorish trick of using olives, almonds, raisins and apples. However the true soul of Mexican soup is gained, as it is in most of their other foods, from the *recaudo*, or basic sauce of tomato and onion.

The French maintain that the only way to confect a civilized soup or sauce is in an earthenware pot; a Mexican cook may be short on theory, but she uses only a clay *olla* or *cazuela* for *salsa* or *sopa*. In soup making, Mexican style, the *recaudo* is made in a clay *cazuela*, then when the other ingredients are added the soup retains its most delicate flavor nuances. A nest of four or five *cazuelas*, called a *juego* or game, costs less than a dollar in Mexican markets, and many Americans bring back a *juego* for use and atmosphere.

To ready a *recaudo*, heat three tablespoons of peanut oil to a mild warmth, so the vegetables won't blacken. Drop in finely chopped onions and garlic with peeled, sliced chiles and slowly sauté them until the onion is a light golden color. Peeled, mashed tomatoes are stirred in with salt and pepper and cooked until tender.

The versatile *recaudo* is ready to use in a number of ways. It may be poured over a hot dish that has been prepared separately, such as ranch-style eggs, *chiles rellenos*, or baked fish. On the other hand it may be added to a fish or roast which is then baked or stewed until it picks up the genuine rancho flavor. Many soups, both liquid and dry, are built around the sturdy *recaudo*.

Herbs are frequently added to the *recaudo;* coriander and *orégano* are generally the front runners in popularity with Mexican cooks. In central and southern Mexico fresh coriander is used so prodigally that it overpowers the food for the average gringo taste.

One or more types of chile are always found in the *recaudo*. Spiciness is not the purpose in cooking with chiles; the aim is to capture the individual flavor stored in each capsicum pod. Mexico has dozens of varieties that are not available in this country, so I have usually suggested a touch of cayenne or chili powder for piquancy, and chopped sweet pepper or pimiento for the exotic flavor.

In Mexico one sees the small green peppers, called *chile verde*, in all the markets. This type is used almost exclusively for *salsa*, a raw sauce of chile, tomato and onion. *Chile poblano*, which is widely used, is similar to our sweet or bell pepper. *Ancho, cora* and *chilcate* are used in dry form only; the *ancho* is the pepper from which chili powder is ground, and *cora* is similar to the small dry cayenne peppers found in our stores. *Chipotle* and *jalapeño* are very popular; they are canned and may be bought in the United States along with bottled wax and green peppers. Never forget that all chiles are natural digestive stimulants, and that they are the highest vitamin producers among the vegetables.

Mexican cooks go heavy on pork fat, and it is this lard that frequently leads to stomach upset among tourists rather than the food itself. Mexican foods, aside from beans, are usually light. I suggest peanut oil for most Mexican dishes. Raw or canned tomatoes should be used for soups and *salsas*, but I have recommended tomato sauce for most other recipes. However, if you have a stone *molcajete* and wish to go native by grinding your own tomatoes and chile, then *buena suerte, amigo.*

Albóndigas (MEAT BALL SOUP)

Albóndigas is like a pretty girl with brains; it has everything you're looking for as well as unexpected and tantalizing side effects An *olla* of *albóndigas* with very little help from the sideboard will make a meal that is at once complete, exotic and satisfying. Whenever you serve this dish make plenty of meat balls, because they are so good your guests will smuggle out half a dozen in their dinner jackets to nibble on the way home.

Mexican housewives take unlimited liberties with this amiable soup: Some hide a stuffed green olive in each meat ball, and others core the *albóndiga* with a wedge of boiled egg or chopped nuts. In cooler weather I like to hearten the soup with a cup of dry macaroni.

1 large can solid pack tomatoes	½ tsp. ground oregano
2 qts. water	Salt, pepper, Cayenne
1 clove garlic	½ lb. ground beef
2 onions, chopped	½ lb. lean ground sausage
2 fresh green chile peppers	1 cup corn meal
1 tbs. cooking oil	2 eggs
1 tsp. chili powder	

Put tomatoes and water to boil. Sauté garlic, *one* onion and *one* chopped, seeded chile in oil. Add chili powder and one half cup soup water to vegetables. Stir until smooth and add to soup. Season with *one quarter* teaspoon oregano, salt, and Cayenne. Continue simmering.

To make meat balls combine meat, the other onion, the other chile pepper, seeded and chopped, one quarter teaspoon oregano, salt, corn meal and eggs. Mix by hand for at least ten minutes until everything is incorporated. Gently pat out *albóndigas* the size of walnuts and drop into soup. Cook for another hour.

Rally eight people of good taste around and serve soup in large bowls with toasted French bread and fresh *salsa*.

Sopa de Arroz (RICE SOUP)

Sopa de arroz is one of the most authentically Mexican dishes one could use as a sideboy at a Mexican dinner or barbecue. It makes no demands of its own and amiably supports any dish you can put with it.

It is usually necessary for a cook to prepare *sopa de arroz* two or three times to gain complete mastery, but once the knack is learned this dish can be varied dozens of ways to suit individual taste.

Mexican cooks usually fry the dry rice first in deep fat, but I recommend sautéing it in two tablespoons of peanut oil over low heat. Stir frequently and take at least five minutes for the kernels to turn the lightest golden color. If you insist on washing the rice first then dry it thoroughly before dropping into the pan.

The second phase of gaining virtuosity is to put in the exact amount of liquid, so the rice will cook done and each grain will be fluffy and separate. Give a cooking time of thirty minutes without once lifting the lid. If the rice is still hard, there was too little liquid; if it is still soupy, there was too much.

½ lb. dry rice	2 cloves garlic, mashed
2 tbs. peanut oil	Salt and pepper
1 small onion, chopped	1 qt. soup stock

Sauté the dry rice in oil over low heat for five minutes, then add the onion and garlic and give it another five minutes. Add salt and pepper and soup stock, cover tightly and finish cooking over lowest heat for half an hour.

This is a basic *sopa de arroz* for eight people. You may add each or all of the following; it seems impossible to overdo.

Raw or canned mushrooms	Chunks of chicken
Chopped parsley	Chopped sweet pepper
Shrimp	1 small hot pepper
Crab	Hamburger
Lobster	Tomato juice

Sauté everything but seafood with the onions. Use the liquid from canned ingredients, but keep the total to a quart.

To make *sopa de arroz casera*, or family style, use one third tomato juice, two thirds soup stock, a cup of peas and half a cooked potato, sectioned. *Sopa de arroz arriero*, or mule skinner's rice soup is made by adding three skinned and chopped *chorizos* to the basic recipe.

Arroz Margarita (RICE MARGARET)

Rice Margaret is a universal favorite; no one can resist its delicate nuances of savor and sheer succulent goodness, yet there is never a *sospecho* of spice to pique the most gentle of palates.

1 frying chicken cut into serving pieces	15 pitted black olives
Oil for frying	1 tbs. capers
3 slices raw ham, chopped	5 cups *sopa de arroz* (see recipe)
3 slices bacon, chopped	1 pt. fresh cream
2 tbs. chopped onion	1 can tomato sauce
Salt and pepper	3 slices salami

Fry the chicken quickly on both sides, pour off the oil and save; add water, cover and cook until chicken is done.

In the oil fry the chopped ham and bacon. Sauté the onion and add tomato sauce, and simmer until sauce thickens; salt and pepper.

Cover the bottom of a casserole with rice and nest the chicken in it; add the ham, bacon, olives and capers. Over the rice pour the onion-tomato sauce mix and cream mixed, arrange slices of salami, dot with butter and place in a 450° oven for fifteen minutes to heat and incorporate the ingredients. Serves four.

Arroz con Jamón (RICE-HAM SOUP)

Don't be fooled, this is another dry soup and will be served either in the *pasta* or the main course.

1 cup dry rice	Salt and pepper
¼ lb. chopped, cooked ham	3 eggs
1 bell pepper, chopped fine	Bread crumbs
12 pitted olives, chopped	Grated Cheddar cheese
1 tsp. chopped parsley	Butter
1 tsp. chopped onion	

Cook the rice either Mexican style or boiled.

Butter the inside of a shallow casserole and line the sides and bottom with cooked rice.

Make a filling by mixing the ham, pepper, olives, onion, parsley and seasonings and work in the beaten eggs.

Fill the rice with the mixture and cover with bread crumbs, grated cheddar cheese and small dabs of butter.

Cook covered in a preheated 250° oven for half an hour.

Arroz con Piña (EXOTIC RICE)

Morelos is a small but fascinating state just over the Sierra from Mexico City. Morelos has a wide range of climates and an equally wide selection of products. The state has been growing rice, its chief staple, for well over 400 years. As a matter of fact, it produces more rice than the rest of the Republic.

Here is a perfect *pasta*, blending the state's typical goodies, that is one of the specialties of Cuautla of the hot baths.

1 ½ cups rice	⅛ tsp. ground clove
½ cup pineapple juice	1 ½ tbs. wine vinegar
2 ½ cups ground, cooked ham	2 tbs. brown sugar
⅓ cup chopped sweet pepper	1 ½ tsps. prepared mustard
2 tsps. cooking oil	Salt and pepper

Sauté the rice gently in oil until it barely changes color, then add half the pineapple juice and enough water to barely cover. Bring to boil and immediately cut to lowest heat and cook covered until dry, approximately half an hour.

In a separate dish sauté the ham and sweet pepper; then add the other ingredients, including the remaining pineapple juice, and cook slowly for 12 minutes.

Turn out the rice on a platter and serve the sauce over the top. Everything needs to be hot at moment of serving. Six helpings.

Arroz Pompeya (RICE POMPEY)

Serve Rice Pompey as a *pasta* course when you plan a real blowout. The dish requires a little more preparation than other rice soups, but it is definitely outstanding in looks and savor.

1 ½ cups dry rice	2 slices cooked ham, ground
Peanut or olive oil	2 tbs. finely chopped parsley
2 tbs. chili powder	2 tbs. capers
1 qt. chicken stock	2 fried chorizos, chopped,
2 cloves garlic, crushed	or pork sausage
2 tbs. finely chopped onions	2 hard cooked eggs,
Salt	chopped fine

Sauté the rice; then stir in the chili powder diluted in a couple spoonsful of chicken stock. Now add the garlic and onions; salt, and pour in the soup stock. Stir well and cover tightly. Cook until rice is dry and fluffy, but don't lift the lid for at least thirty minutes. Keep heat low and it won't burn.

When done, spoon enough rice into a buttered casserole to cover bottom. The rest of the ingredients are mixed, and a layer is spooned over the rice. Make alternate layers, ending with a layer of ham-sausage filler on top.

Dot the top with butter and bake quickly and lightly to glaze. This is known as the "Last Glaze of Pompey." Enough for six.

Caldo de Arroz con Pollo (CHICKEN RICE SOUP)

Here is a chicken-rice soup such as you have never tasted. It is a specialty of the mile-and-a-half high mountain cities of Zacatecas and Durango, and it combines everything a Mexican food *aficionado* loves: savor, body and greenery on top. Observe the compatibility.

2 qts. chicken soup	2 chicken livers, cooked
1 ½ cups white rice	and chopped
2 cups fresh chopped or solid	1 chicken gizzard, cooked
pack tomatoes	and chopped
3 tbs. finely chopped onion	2 tbs. capers
1 clove garlic, pressed	2 hard cooked eggs,
1 tbs. finely chopped parsley	finely chopped
Salt and pepper	

Bring the stock to a boil and stir in the rice. When it is cooking happily, add the tomato, onion, garlic, parsley, salt and pepper. After the soup has cooked ten minutes, add everything but the chopped eggs. Cook until the rice is done, approximately thirty minutes.

Pour the soup into a tureen, sprinkle the chopped eggs on top and serve eight.

Caldillo de Carne Seca (DRIED MEAT SOUP)

This savory, pick-me-up soup is a favorite with cowboys, sportsmen on the morning after and honeymooners. It alerts the stomach, steadies the pulse, and puts new light in the eyes.

½ lb. dried meat	2 pickled wax peppers or
1 tsp. cooking oil	drop Tabasco sauce
1 onion	1 large tomato
2 cloves garlic	1 tbs. cornstarch
½ bell pepper, chopped	2 ½ cups water
	Salt, pepper and thyme

Chop or grind the meat as minutely as possible. Sauté the onion, garlic, meat and peppers, add the tomato and cook five minutes.

Mix the cornstarch in a cup of water and add to *recaudo* with rest of the water. Sprinkle in a teaspoon of thyme, and salt and pepper to taste. Cook ten mi utes and serve with well toasted tortillas. Plenty for four.

Caldo de Elote Guadalajara
(GUADALAJARA CORN SOUP)

The cook who shared her delicate soup secret with me used a good deal of courage in compounding the *caldo*; she courageously stayed away from the chile bin and the garlic jar. This soup displays true Mexican character; its suaveness and individuality are found nowhere but in the Republic.

2 tbs. butter	3 cups hot milk
1 cup sweet corn kernels,	⅛ tsp. nutmeg
1 tbs. flour	Salt and pepper

Sauté the kernels lightly in one tablespoon of butter, and then cook quickly in salted water. If canned corn is used the second step is omitted.

Put the drained corn through a food chopper, reserving cooking water, and refry lightly, mixing in a tablespoon of flour which has been sautéed to a delicate straw color. At no time allow corn to harden or discolor.

Stir in the milk, which is hot but not boiled, and the water in which the corn was cooked. Salt, pepper and nutmeg to taste. Serves four.

Caldo de Habas Secas (BROAD BEAN SOUP)

The broad bean is an interesting old friend of the human race. It was grown by the Chinese at least five thousand years ago and has leisurely traveled the entire earth.

The Romans called the legume "*faba*", under which name it migrated to English speaking countries. However the Spanish language naturalized it to "*haba*."

The *faba* is not a lima bean, but don't hesitate to substitute limas if broad beans are unavailable. Either way you cook it, the soup is the essence of Spanish Mexico.

½ lb. broad beans
  1 small onion chopped
  1 clove garlic, chopped
  1 sprig mint

Salt and pepper
  1 large, chopped tomato
  3 tsps. olive oil

Put the beans on to cook in three pints of water with the garlic, onion, mint and salt.

Sauté the tomato in one teaspoon olive oil, pepper and add to the beans when they are almost done. At the moment of serving mix in the rest of the olive oil.

This soup is served either thick or thin, according to preference. Four generous bowls.

Cocido Madrileño (MADRID FEAST)

Cocido Madrileño is one of those Mexican versions of the New England boiled dinners in which a multiplicity of good foods supplement and compliment each other.

½ lb. garbanzos	1 large onion
½ lb. navy beans	1 chorizo (optional)
1 tender boiling chicken	1 small, firm cabbage
1 lb. beef heart	2 lbs. medium potatoes
¼ lb. lean, unsliced bacon	Salt and pepper
¼ lb. uncooked ham	

Soak the beans and garbanzos overnight in separate containers.

In a ceramic pot of at least seven quart capacity put the chicken and all the meats except chorizo (unsliced), chopped onion, beans and salt and pepper. Tie the garbanzos in a white cloth bag that has been thoroughly washed and bury it in the pot. Cover with five or six quarts of water.

Time the covered pot, and when it has boiled five hours add the chorizos if you desire them. Pull six leaves from the cabbage, chop fine and add to the soup. Toss in the rest of the cabbage whole. Cube four potatoes fine to add body to the soup and roll in the remaining peeled potatoes whole.

Cook another forty minutes and serve.

To serve pour the soup in a tureen with the beans, potatoes, and cabbage. Mexicans love to see floating greenery such as spinach, coriander or even lettuce in their soups. You don't have to do it that way, if it offends you.

On a large platter offer the disjointed chicken and sliced meat. The garbanzos go into another bowl.

This feast calls for guacamole and lots of red *salsa*. Serves eight handsomely.

Crema de Espárragos (ASPARAGUS CREAM SOUP)

The custom is to serve sliced avocado and fresh limes with this soup.

1 lb. cooked asparagus	2 eggs
2 qts. milk	½ cup cream
2 tsps. corn starch	Salt and pepper
2 tsps. butter	

Grind the cooked asparagus, pour in the milk and heat until a faint steam is breathed off. Put through collander.

In the melted butter heat the corn starch, but don't let it discolor. Slowly stir in the asparagus-milk purée, salt and pepper. Simmer until the purée thickens slightly, then add the eggs beaten in the cream, and the rest of the butter. Makes eight servings.

Gazpacho (COLD SOUP)

When the tropical sun is high, and the afternoon breezes haven't yet started the palm fronds whispering, it is pleasant to sit on a terrace overlooking an unruffled bay and to contemplate a *gazpacho*. The chilled fruit and vegetables flatter the palate and further soothe the spirit.

1 large can tomato juice
2 large tender cucumbers, peeled and sliced thin
1 avocado, peeled and chopped
1 bell pepper, chopped fine

1 tsp. olive oil
1 tsp. lime or lemon juice
½ tsp. Lea & Perrins sauce
Salt and pepper

Mix everything thoroughly and leave in the refrigerator until it is thoroughly chilled. *Gazpacho* may be varied by stirring in two envelopes of gelatin and hardening. Serves four lotus eaters.

Menudo Morelia (MORELIA TRIPE SOUP)

Morelia is a gracious old city which has retained the dignified tempo of colonial Mexico. A high, brown-stone aqueduct, built by the viceroys, strides into town on soaring arches, and the cathedral's mellow chimes call the time every quarter hour.

Across the street from the cathedral is the Oseguerra Hotel, a hostelry whose old-fashioned entrance hides tile paved patios, plashing fountains and a superb restaurant.

Menudo is a favorite of Mexicans all over the country, but the *menudo* of Morelia captures the soothing flavor of a city that has moved, leisurely and unhurried, for more than four centuries. In the kitchen of the Oseguerra the master *menudo* of all is brewed.

3 lbs. tripe
2 calves' feet
2 chopped onions
2 cloves garlic, mashed
2 cups hominy
2 qts. water

1 tsp. oregano
⅛ tsp. each thyme & cinnamon
Pinch ground cloves
Salt and pepper
1 small can Vienna sausage

Cook the calves' feet in salted water for an hour and then add slivered tripe and all the other ingredients, except the sausage. Cook for five hours and add the sausages. Simmer an additional hour. Enough for six persons.

Potaje de Frijol Blanco (WHITE BEAN POTTAGE)

It is clear that Tlaloc, the Aztec nature god, intended beans to be the birthright of his people, because both Mexicans and *frijoles* originated in Mexico. Beans are found in every color from white through pink, brown, red, yellow and black; they are speckled, dappled, striped and painted, yet each *frijol* has its own purpose and area. In the hot country the people eat black beans. Across the northern desert the "fat bay," or *bayo gordo*, is favored, and in the high, cold country the white bean gives warmth and energy.

The next time you get ready to carry eighty pounds of pottery over a seven thousand foot mountain to the Friday market, fortify yourself and three friends with this high octane soup.

½ lb. white beans	½ sweet pepper, chopped
Salt	1 slice ham, chopped
½ leg of pork	2 chorizos or pork sausages
Cooking oil	1 can tomato sauce
1 onion, chopped	1 slice cabbage ¼″ thick

Wash beans thoroughly and soak all night. Put them on to cook in same water and add salt two hours later. When you add salt start the chopped pork cooking in salted, boiling water.

Half an hour later heat two tablespoons of oil in a large *cazuela* or casserole and sauté the onion, pepper, ham and the skinned and chopped chorizos or sausage. Add tomato sauce and bring to a boil.

Now pour in the beans and meat with all the liquid, drop in the cabbage and simmer for two hours until the pottage thickens. The cabbage is put in for nothing but decoration. Serves six.

Potaje de Garbanzos (CHICK PEA POTTAGE)

Garbanzos are one of the ancient and honorable legumes which were cultivated long before the Christian era. They were brought to Mexico by the Spaniards, where they supplement rather than compete with the *frijol*. The two vegetables are frequently cooked together.

1 lb. garbanzos	2 cloves
2 bay leaves	2 tbs. cooking oil
1 sprig parsley	3 hard cooked egg yolks
2 medium onions	Salt and pepper

Soak the garbanzos over night and put on to cook with the bay leaves, parsley and one whole onion stuck with the cloves.

Chop the other onion and sauté. Drain and grind with the onion that was cooked in the garbanzos. Grind half of the cooked garbanzos and the cooked egg yolks.

Stir everything into the whole garbanzo soup; add salt and pepper. It is well to salt any kind of beans after they have cooked a while, because salt tends to keep them hard.

One serves quarters of fried bread with this. Serves four.

Pozole (PORK AND HOMINY SOUP)

Bucareli Avenue in Mexico City joins world-famous Paseo de la Reforma at the statue of the little horse. If one walks up Bucareli, he is quickly absorbed by the authentic blood stream of the capital.

Here is Mexico at its best and here are dozens of modern cafes listing every dish served from Chihuahua to Yucatan. Probably the one dish that is purveyed by all and featured by many is the savory, heartening soup called *pozole*. Many a worker keeps his energy up and his weight down with this high protein, low caloried ambrosia.

1 lb. farmer style pork ribs, chopped	1 qt. water
*1 lb. cubed lean pork	1 lb. canned hominy
1 large onion	2 tsps. chili powder
1 clove garlic	Salt and pepper

*(I use 2 lbs. of pork ribs and no other meat.)

Cook the pork, onion and garlic in salted water until meat is tender. Add hominy with its water and cook another hour. Twenty minutes before serving add chili powder.

Pozole wants to be very soupy and served hot with chopped green onions and garlic French bread. A main dish for eight.

Puré de Garbanzos (CHICK PEA SOUP)

The flavor that distinguishes this purée comes from the Mexican herb bouquet, called *hierbas de olor*. Tie together a bay leaf and a sprig each of thyme, marjoram and oregano to make the savory herb bouquet. If leaves are not available use a pinch each of the ground herbs.

1 lb. garbanzos	2 slices bacon
1 medium onion	3 cups beef broth
2 small, crisp carrots	*Hierbas de olor*

Soak the garbanzos over night. Put them on to cook with the whole vegetables, bacon and *hierbas de olor*. Cook slowly and stir now and then to prevent sticking; about four hours will be necessary. Add broth if purée thickens too fast.

When the garbanzos are completely soft, lift out the bacon, *hierbas de olor* and vegetables and put the garbanzos through a colander. Salt, reheat and serve with toasted hard rolls or garlic French bread. Serves four.

Puré de Legumbres (VEGETABLE PUREE)

This is an unpretentious soup of humble origin. However it has sturdy character, good looks and a heart-warming approach.

2 qts. navy bean purée	1 tsp. cornstarch
Cooking oil	1 lb. spinach, chard or
1 large onion	turnip greens
1 large, ripe tomato	Salt and pepper

Run a pot of cooked navy beans through a coarse colander that takes out only the hulls.

Sauté the onion and add the peeled tomato well chopped. Add the cornstarch which has been mixed with a little water. Stir in the bean purée, well chopped greens, salt and pepper. Cover and simmer for half an hour.

Have plenty of red *salsa* and hot garlic rolls to accompany the *frijoles*. Serves eight.

Sopa de Ajo (GARLIC SOUP)

I would hesitate to offer this recipe, because its name will immediately make it suspect, if it weren't for its honorable and classic place in the Mexican cuisine. One can only guess at its antiquity, and, until he has tasted it, one can only guess at its delicate flavor. Many visitors to Mexico have eaten *sopa de ajo* and thought they were enjoying a delicate potato soup.

10 cloves garlic
½ tsp. flour
2 tbs. butter
1 qt. strained beef or
  chicken stock
Few drops Tabasco

Salt and pepper
4 eggs
2 tbs. finely crumbled
  white cheese
1 tbs. chopped parsley

Mash garlic as fine as possible, add flour and sauté in butter, using clay pot. Add the soup stock and boil fifteen minutes. Strain and return to fire. Add seasonings. With the soup at a boil slip the eggs in gently, one at a time, so the yolk doesn't break. When the eggs are poached serve the soup with one egg in each bowl and parsley and cheese sprinkled over the top. Four portions.

Sopa de Avena (OATMEAL SOUP)

½ cup breakfast oats
4 cups broth or bouillon
½ cup cream

Salt and pepper
1 egg yolk
¼ cup grated cheese

Sauté the oats slowly in melted butter; add broth, salt and pepper and cook twenty minutes.

When ready to serve stir in the cream and beaten eggs yolk and sprinkle cheese on top. Serves four.

Sopa de Bolitas de Arroz (RICE BALL SOUP)

1 qt. chicken soup
1½ cups cold, cooked rice
2 eggs

Nutmeg
Salt and pepper

Grind the cooked rice and mix in slightly beaten eggs, salt, pepper and nutmeg. Form into balls the size of walnuts.

Bring the chicken soup to a boil and drop in rice balls; cook ten minutes and serve.

Sopa de Bolitas de Tortilla
(TORTILLA DUMPLING SOUP)

6 fresh tortillas	1 clove garlic
1 cup milk	½ onion
2 eggs	1 can tomato sauce
Salt and pepper	Yolk of hard-boiled egg
1 tbs. flour	3 pts. meat stock
Butter	

Soak the tortillas four hours in milk; remove them and grind in food chopper. To the tortilla paste add two beaten eggs, salt and pepper and enough flour to firm the paste so it can be formed into dumplings the size of chestnuts. Fry the dumplings in melted butter and set apart.

Sauté the chopped onion and garlic in butter, add the tomato sauce and cook five minutes. Now stir in the yolk of a hard cooked egg grated fine and let the *recaudo* cool.

Add the meat stock to the *recaudo* and bring to a boil. Drop in the dumplings and cook five to ten minutes, but don't let them start to fall apart. Plenty for four.

Sopa de Cacahuate (PEANUT SOUP)

If you find yourself working for peanuts, try this provender. You will be surprised by its sturdy character and full, creamy flavor.

1 cup cleaned, toasted peanuts	2 tsps. brown sugar
1 tsp. butter	(adjust to taste)
2 cups hot water	Salt
	1 glass dry sherry
	1 can evaporated milk

Grind peanuts and toast a few seconds in melted butter; pour in a cup of hot water and add sugar and salt. Cook slowly for fifteen minutes.

Just before serving add the milk and sherry—and another cup of boiling water if thinner consistency is preferred.

Serve with slices of bread fried in olive oil to four gourmets.

Sopa de Calabaza (SUMMER SQUASH SOUP)

Here is a heartening soup that will lie gently on the stomach and help chase away the evil humors on a hot summer day. It is compounded of the best summer vegetables, yet so smoothly blended that even children don't realize they are eating what is good for them.

1 medium onion, chopped	Salt and pepper
1 lb. tomatoes, peeled & chopped	4 chicken livers cooked and
2 tbs. flour	well chopped
2 tbs. butter	2 egg yolks
1 lb. cooked zucchini or	1 pt. cream
summer squash	1 cup cooked green peas
3 pts. chicken broth	

Sauté the onion and tomato until the onion is tender, then press through colander. Heat the flour in melted butter but don't let it change color; add the tomato and onion, cooked squash, chicken broth, salt and pepper. Boil gently for fifteen minutes.

Blend the chicken liver and egg yolks with the cream and pour into a soup tureen. Add the cooked peas and pour in the squash soup. Stir well and serve. Eight hearty servings.

Sopa de Cebolla (ONION CREAM SOUP)

6 large onions	2 doz. small green olives
Cooking oil	1 small can pimientos
1 tbs. flour	1 tsp. Lea & Perrins sauce
½ pt. fresh cream	Salt and pepper
3 pints milk	

In one tablespoon butter sauté the onion, garlic, tomato, parsley and cauliflower, chopped very fine. Stir in the salt and oregano and cook five minutes.

In a ceramic soup vessel heat the other spoon of butter and stir in the flour; toast it but don't allow it to brown.

Now pour the sautéed vegetables into the pot, stir well and add soup stock. Cook slowly for twenty minutes.

Just before serving stir in the grated cheese and cook a few minutes until it incorporates thoroughly. Eight servings.

Sopa de Crema (MEAT BALLS WITH CREAM SOUP)

The Carmelite nuns of Santa Teresa in Puebla were famous for this soup in the days of the viceroys. The convent and its large kitchen have been closed for more than a century, but the Poblanos continue to brew from the secret formula and declare there is non-such anywhere else.

2 large onions, chopped	Salt and pepper
1 slice bread	1 tbs. flour
Milk	1 qt. chicken stock
1 egg	1 tbs. chopped parsley
½ lb. ground round	Wine glass sherry

Cook the onions, covered, for half an hour in salted boiling water; mash through colander.

Soak the bread quickly in milk and grind or mash with fork. Mix the bread, a beaten egg, meat, salt and pepper and form into small balls the size of filberts.

Heat the onion soup and stir in paste made of flour mixed with a little water; add chicken stock and bring to boil. Drop in meat balls and chopped parsley, salt lightly, and just before serving pour in the sherry. Serves four.

Sopa del Curato (SOUP FOR THE CURATE'S VISIT)

When the curate paid his weekly visit to the convent of Santa Teresa in Puebla, the sisters bustled about the *cocina* preparing food just the way the father liked it. This is it.

1 qt. beef stock	1 tsp. flour
1 lb. ripe tomatoes	1 tbs. chopped parsley
Salt	2 cups bread croutons cut in
3 tbs. chopped onions	circles
1 tsp. sugar	2 eggs, separated
Butter	Grated Parmesan cheese

Be sure there is not a speck of grease in the soup stock and start it heating. Add the peeled and chopped tomatoes, salt, and onion; simmer for an hour. Rub the soup through a sieve and return to fire.

Add a heaping teaspoon of sugar, a tablespoon of butter rolled in flour, salt and pepper. Simmer five minutes and serve with croutons.

To make the croutons cut tiny circles from the bread until you have two cups full. Beat the egg yolk and whip the whites stiff; fold in the whites and dip the bread rounds in the egg. Sprinkle with cheese and fry in butter.

At moment of serving sprinkle a little powdered cheese and chopped parsley over the soup and delicately introduce the croutons. Enough for four pilgrims.

Sopa de Gallina y Almendra
(CHICKEN AND ALMOND SOUP)

The nunneries of Mexico have been closed for many years, but here and there some of their famous recipes, written in a delicate, feathery script, are still preserved.

The nuns of Santa Teresa in Puebla specialized in soups that were as unhurried, judicious and tasteful as their own days. Just before serving this soup drink a light, meditative white wine, bless the dish with a brief *"buen provecho"* and the food will lighten your stomach, sweeten your disposition and make more modest your demeanor.

1 uncooked chicken breast	2 tbs. chopped parsley
1 pt. clear beef broth, home	Cooking oil
cooked or canned	1 egg yolk
3 slices bread	¼ lb. almond nuts
Milk	1 tbs. finely ground walnuts

Cook half the chicken breast in the broth. While it simmers grind the other half-chicken breast with a slice of stale bread soaked in milk. Mix in one tablespoon finely chopped parsley, half a teaspoon of cooking oil, an egg yolk and a tiny sprinkle of salt.

When the chicken in the soup is tender, remove it and grind with the almonds which have been toasted. Add one tablespoon of chopped parsley and the walnuts ground to a powder. Strain the soup and return the chicken, parsley and walnuts to the broth.

Make tiny *albóndigas*, or balls the size of marbles from the raw chicken breast, bread, parsley and egg yolk and drop gently into the soup. Salt sparingly and cook slowly for half an hour.

Have hot croutons ready, drop them into the soup tureen and pour the soup over them. Serves four.

Sopa de Hígado (LIVER SOUP)

Mexican foods frequently serve two or three purposes; they are not only alimentation, but they may serve to ward off or cure all sorts of ailments. Over ninety percent of Mexico's cities lie at altitudes ranging from five to nine thousand feet, so it is patent one should take steps to combat mountain sickness.

Sopa de hígado is the panacea for *mal de sierra*, and the ideal proving ground is Toluca, some fifty miles from Mexico City. Toluca, at an altitude of 8500 feet, weaves most of Mexico's baskets and displays tens of thousands of the stout *canastas*, each Friday.

For the busy basket buyer who has spent a morning walking, viewing and haggling, nothing puts heart back into him as quickly as a bowl of the delicate yet fortifying *sopa de hígado*; it tightens up the reins, lightens the lungs and melts the rubber out of the legs.

1 lb. cooked liver	2 qts. beef stock
Oil for frying	Salt and pepper
2 tbs. cooking oil	1 wine glass sherry
2 tbs. flour	

Fry the liver quickly on each side then cover and cook over low heat for fifteen minutes; cool, wipe dry and grind fine.

In a clay or ceramic pot heat the oil and brown the flour. Add the soup and stir until smooth; introduce the liver, salt and pepper and simmer ten minutes. Pour in the libation of wine just before serving. With toasted Mexican or French bread it fortifies eight persons.

Sopa de Jericaya

This soup is as exotically excellent as ambrosia floated in nectar, and it will dissipate dull care like a double decker lotus sandwich.

4 eggs	1 tsp. sugar, caramelized
2 qts. chicken broth	¼ cup wine
1 tsp. flour	
Salt, pepper and nutmeg to taste	

Put the beaten eggs in a double boiler and slowly stir in one cup cool broth and flour; flavor with salt, pepper and nutmeg. Cover and cook until the *jericaya* thickens.

Heat the broth and, just before serving, add sugar and sherry. Cut the *jericaya* into four pieces, place them in soup dishes and pour the soup over.

Sopa de Lentejas y Tocino
(LENTIL AND BACON SOUP)

Lentil soup is a Mediterranean dish that was old when the Bible was written; Jacob swapped Essau bread and a pottage of lentils for his birthright. However the red lentil had to wait many centuries to join the Mexican tomato and gain the suavity this pottage enjoys today.

¼ lb. lentils	1 can tomato sauce
Salt and pepper	2 qts. soup stock
3 slices bacon cut fine	2 egg yolks
2 onions chopped	¼ cup pimiento strips

Cook lentils for one hour in a pint and a half of water with salt and pepper.

Fry bacon lightly and remove from pan. In the bacon fat sauté the onion, add the tomato sauce and simmer ten minutes. Now mix the lentils, bacon, soup stock and tomato *recaudo*, and simmer another forty-five minutes.

Just before serving, remove soup pot from stove. Beat the two egg yolks in a cup of the soup and add to the lentils. Stir in the pimiento and serve hot.

Hard rolls, of course, have to go with it. Serves eight.

Sopa de Manzana (APPLE SOUP)

On the seven and eight thousand foot plateaus of the state of Puebla apple orchards cover the land. Around the capital city of Puebla, and in the tiny village of Acaxochitlán, on the northern border, barrels of cider, apple wine, brandy and champagne are compounded with loving care. Any time a cook in this region passes a boiling pot she tosses in an apple or a glass of apple wine.

Wine is used in cooking to sharpen and to enrich natural flavors. The alcohol volatilizes and floats away well below boiling point. This apple soup is a great specific against the night chill; it is greater when it is preceded by a glass of applejack.

½ chopped onion	1½ firm apples, peeled and
2 tbs. butter	chopped
1 tbs. flour	1 small glass apple wine
½ cup tomato juice	or sherry
1 qt. soup stock	1 tbs. chopped parsley
Salt and pepper	

Sauté the onion in butter, add flour and stir until it barely changes color; then add the tomato juice and simmer for five minutes.

Pour in soup stock, add salt and pepper, and simmer ten minutes, covered. Remove from stove, add apples in small cubes and sherry. Garnish with chopped parsley and serve four.

Sopa de Nueces (WALNUT SOUP)

3½ pints soup stock	½ can evaporated milk
10 walnut meats, ground	4 tbs. flour mixed with
2 tbs. finely chopped onion	water to paste
Salt and pepper	2 egg yolks

Heat the soup and add the ground walnuts, onion, salt and pepper; cook slowly for half an hour.

Add the milk and stir in the flour which has been made into a smooth paste with cold water. Simmer another five minutes.

Beat the eggs and pour into soup tureen and pour in hot soup.

Sip slowly and meditate on your *pecadillos*. Enough for eight.

Sopa de Papa (POTATO SOUP SUPREME)

Before you flip over this recipe and label it just another potato pottage, stop, look and glisten. It took the discovery of Peru, the genius of Spain and the imagination of Mexico to confect this creamy collation.

The masterly use of three alliums—leeks, garlic and onion—gives the potion an indescribable *yo no sé qué*.

5 medium potatoes	1 tbs. chopped onion
2 tbs. butter	1 small clove garlic, chopped
1 whole leek sliced thin	Salt and pepper
1 can tomato sauce	1 qt. chicken broth

Peel the potatoes and slice lengthwise in very thin strips. Melt the butter in a ceramic pot and sauté potatoes and leek until transparent but not singed. Add the tomato, onion, garlic, salt and pepper. Cook five minutes. Now pour in the broth and cook until potatoes are tender. Four healthy helpings.

Sopa de Patitas de Puerco (LITTLE PIG FEET SOUP)

Your prejudice will try to make you duck this one, but go ahead and live dangerously. Confect an *olla* of this delicate stomach tonic, and you will find it smoother than a silk purse made from a sow's hoof.

1 chopped onion	2 large potatoes, chopped
1 clove garlic, chopped	½ cup tomato sauce
1 pimiento, sliced	1 egg yolk
3 bell peppers, chopped	Salt and pepper
3 pig's feet	½ cup sherry
2 tsp. cooking oil	

In three quarts of water cook the onion, garlic, peppers and pig's feet until the meat falls off the bone. Remove bones, skin and fat and leave only lean meat in the soup.

Sauté the cubed potatoes until golden. Add the tomato sauce and cook five more minutes.

Pour in the soup and cook twenty more minutes. Remove the garlic and sliced pimiento. Beat the egg yolk in wine and stir into soup just before serving.

Serve chopped green onions, hot sauce, white cheese and white wine as background. Eight servings.

Sopa de Perejil (PARSLEY SOUP)

Mexicans love to play up the diminutive. They call the equestrian statue of Carlos IV, who sits astride a giant bronze horse in the Capital, the "little horse," but a baby is referred to as the "big man." In giving directions or distances it is common to say a place is "a tiny, long-ways off."

Parsley soup is really a potato soup in which the loved greenery is given the spot. It is equivalent to a piccolo solo in a symphony orchestra.

Any way you play it, however, this parsley soup proves harmonious and rewarding.

2 sprigs parsley	4 potatoes, cubed
5 cloves garlic	1 qt. beef broth
1 tbs. butter	Salt and pepper
1 tsp. cornstarch	

Chop the parsley and garlic thin, thin. Melt the butter in a casserole and stir in the cornstarch until it is uniform.

Add the parsley and potatoes and sauté lightly until the potatoes are light gold. Now pour in the broth and cook slowly until the potatoes begin to crumble. A Mexican cook told me the soup should be "lightly thick." Serves four.

Sopa de Tortillas con Frijol
(BEAN AND TORTILLA SOUP)

Bean soup is to the Mexican what dry wine is to a Frenchman. Given a blindfold test, the *frijol aficionado* will tell you the bean's vintage, color and the soil altitude at which it was nurtured. The black bean is a national favorite with the states of Vera Cruz and Oaxaca, considered to be the bean Burgundy of Mexico.

Epazote, a red stemmed herb, is included in bean dishes as routinely as we spread butter on bread. *Epazote* is really a weed which thrives in the United States under the aliases of wormseed, santonica or goosefoot. As is true with most Mexican herbs, *epazote* has marvelous side effects, such as treating St. Vitus' dance and warding off fear and the evil effects of night air. The state of Campeche lies next to Oaxaca, Vera Cruz, and Tabasco, and her alert cooks borrowed the best from their neighbors to create tortilla soup.

In a *cazuela* lightly rubbed with butter or oil, fry twelve tortillas cut in thin strips; turn the tortillas often, and when they are light gold in color, add a chopped onion and continue sautéing.

When the onion is tender pour in a quart of bean broth, and add salt, three sprigs of *epazote* and a splash of Tabasco sauce. Boil five minutes, and then set aside for two minutes, tightly covered. Serve sliced limes or lemons with the soup. This makes six portions.

Sopa de Vigilia (SOUP FOR FAST DAYS)

Perhaps the most famous vigil known to literature was that when Don Quixote came to the poor inn and imagined it to be a noble castle. Believing the inn keeper to be high born, Quixote demanded to be dubbed a knight at once. The inn keeper had been around and was one to go along with a gag, so he had Quixote stand vigil in the corral with his sword and shield, over a horse trough.

As the day was Friday the cook had nothing but codfish, which is called *bacalao*, generally, but in La Mancha it was called Little Trout. The sad-faced one sat with his helmet on and ate his *bacalao* with mouldy bread and thin red wine and imagined he was having the regular provender of a nobleman.

The modern vigil-keeper can have the same ingredients in a savory dish fit for the palate of a paladin.

1 cup garbanzos	1 sprig parsley
½ lb. dry codfish	2 bay leaves
2 carrots	¼ tsp. thyme and marjoram
4 tbs. olive oil	½ tsp. oregano
2 cloves garlic	Salt and pepper
2 bunches spinach	2 quarts water
2 cups chopped tomatoes	

Soak the garbanzos and codfish in separate dishes overnight. Next morning put on the chick peas, codfish in small chunks, carrots, one onion and salt. Cook for four hours and take off stove. Mash the carrots and three tablespoons of garbanzos through a colander.

In the oil fry the other onion, which has been well chopped, the garlic and chopped spinach. When everything is tender add the tomatoes and cook five minutes. Now mix the tomato *recaudo* with the mashed carrots, soup, chopped spinach, parsley, bay leaves and seasonings, and cook fifteen minutes. Chop the boiled eggs fine and sprinkle over each bowl of soup when it is served.

Have toasted hard rolls and dry, red wine on the table. Supply each guest with a football helmet so he can imagine he is Don Quixote while he sups. Serves eight.

Sopa Estofada

This easy-to-make soup, which contains the essence of the Mexican rancho, is compounded of the fruits of the country. Approach it and you will smell the smoke of mesquite fires and tortillas toasting on the *comal*.

1 onion, chopped	½ lb. cooked noodles
1 sweet pepper, chopped	20 capers
1 tbs. cooking oil	10 pitted green olives, chopped
2 tomatoes, chopped	2 tbs. seedless raisins
1 qt. soup stock or 6 bouillon cubes in hot water	Dash Tabasco sauce
½ cup sherry wine	Salt and pepper

Sauté the onion and pepper in an earthware pot; add the tomatoes and simmer for five minutes. Pour in the other ingredients and cook slowly for twenty minutes.

Serve with toasted, garlic French bread and fresh *salsa*. For four.

Sopa Mexicana (MEXICAN SOUP)

At first glance it may seem presumptuous for this simple soup to denominate itself the essence of Mexican soupery, as its name implies. However the ingredients and methods add up to what our neighbors refer to as *netamente Mejicana*—netly or one hundred per cent Mexican.

This unpretentious, but savory poor man's soup contains the basic *recaudo* and tortillas; sprinkling cheese over the soup is a national custom, and Juan dearly loves to see finely chopped greenery floating on his *sopa*.

1 tsp. chopped onion	10 tortillas
1 large, ripe tomato, chopped	Salt and pepper
1 tsp. chopped parsley	1 cup shredded white cheese,
Oil for cooking	as crumbly as possible
2 qts. soup stock	
1 cup cooked spinach, well chopped	

Sauté the onion, tomato and parsley until the onion is tender. Add the soup stock and chopped spinach and bring to boil. Drop in the tortillas which have been quartered and lightly fried in deep fat; don't get them too hard.

Serve the soup in bowls and sprinkle on cheese at the last second. Stays eight appetites.

Sopa de Jaiba Luxmar

During a winter I spent in Manzanillo on the Pacific, six fishermen down the beach from my hotel devoted themselves to rebuilding a stout 30-foot boat which they painted blue and named the *Luxmar*. In the early evening when they had finished adzing, planing and shaping, the men would catch a bucket of the succulent blue crabs that like Manzanillo Bay and make a tasty, thick soup.

I frequently joined my friends at crab spearing, and they invited me to enjoy their soup. *Sopa Luxmar* had sturdier character than the frivolous *chipalchole* from Vera Cruz. It was at home with the tangled jungle behind us and the crashing Pacific in front.

A year later Manzanillo was scourged by a hurricane that whipped every boat from the harbor and smashed them to pieces on shore. I saw movies of the destruction and hoped my friends had escaped, even though the beautiful, blue *Luxmar* was gone.

½ onion chopped
2 cloves garlic
3 tbs. cooking oil
1 stalk chopped celery
1 tbs. flour
3 tomatoes chopped

2 qts. fish soup (keep it delicate. 2 small fish heads are best, or a fillet)
1 bell pepper sliced
Meat from 6 crabs
2 potatoes cubed
Salt and pepper

Sauté the onion and garlic; then the celery and flour until all is light gold. Add the tomatoes, broth, pepper strips and potatoes. Cook over a slow fire for twenty minutes then add crab meat. This will feed six persons and a guest.

Sopa de Tortuga (SEA TURTLE SOUP)

The succulent sea turtles of Mexico's Pacific coast live a gracious, leisurely life which allows their meat a chance to season to perfection in the deep blue waters. Turtles live up to two and three hundred years.

For this bolstering soup search for a tender young turtle of one hundred and fifty years. On the other hand, if you don't wish to go out in the deep and arm wrestle a chelonian, cans of turtle meat can be bought in properly conducted markets.

1 can tomato sauce
2 cloves garlic
1 large slice cooked ham
1 tbs. ground almonds
2 tbs. seedless raisins

1 qt. chicken stock
1 lb. turtle meat
1 sprig parsley
Salt and pepper

Combine the tomato sauce, chopped garlic and ham, ground almonds and raisins, and cook for five minutes.

41

Add a quart of skimmed chicken stock, the well chopped turtle meat, raw, and the parsley.

Cook twenty minutes and serve with heated hard rolls.

Sopa Marinera (SAILOR GIRL SOUP)

Ciudad Madero is a fairly good-sized town and a picturesque resort where the vast Panuco River enters the Gulf twelve miles below Tampico. The wide sand beach facing the sea is so firm and even that buses make their regular runs and pickups along the water's edge.

Hotel verandas look out over the Gulf and overhang the levees of the Panuco, and diners sample the world's greatest assortment of seafoods while ocean liners, tankers, tramp steamers and dozens of fishing trawlers hurry up and down the river.

Right on the beach is a large locker building for bathers, and next to it is a sea food restaurant that will serve you anything from turtle to tuna. However, one of their unsung delicacies is a friendly soup that warms the stomach and prepares the diner mentally and physically for the more formidable dishes to come.

1 clove garlic	1 cup finely chopped lobster
2 tbs. butter	Wine glass sherry
2 tbs. flour	Salt and pepper
2 qts. strained soup stock	

Sauté the chopped garlic in butter and remove the garlic; brown the flour lightly and add soup stock. Cook a few minutes, and add the lobster meat.

One minute before serving, pour in the sherry. Have a bowl of garlic butter croutons at hand. For eight.

Sopa Reyna (OYSTER SOUP TO THE QUEEN'S TASTE)

The romantic Gulf of California, which was first named the Sea of Cortés, and later the Vermillion Sea, is the home of the royal pearl oyster. The Aztec emperors and the Spanish rulers received some of their finest gems from the beds near La Paz, and Stein-beck enriched the legend with his story "The Pearl." The Gulf is also the spawning ground of the vicious hurricane called the *chu-basco*. Treasure hunters still search for a pearl-filled caravel of Cortés' which foundered in a *chubasco*.

Hermosillo lies a few miles inland from the gulf and receives tons of seafood daily from Kino Bay. The Queen is long since gone, but her gracious favorite, *Sopa Reyna*, still reigns in Her-mosillo.

1 doz. fresh or canned oysters	2 tbs. butter
1 large *pechuga* (chicken breast) cooked and chopped	2 tbs. flour
	Salt and pepper
1 qt. boiled milk	Pinch bicarbonate of soda
2 tbs. chopped onion	1 tbs. chopped parsley
1 pt. tomato purée	

In a *cazuela*, sauté onions and flour in butter; chop and strain toma-toes and pour juice into *cazuela*; sprinkle in salt and pepper.

When the tomato sauce is blended and simmering, add soda to keep milk from curdling, milk, oysters, cubed chicken and heat two or three minutes. Sprinkle on parsley and serve to four loyal subjects.

Sopa de Cabeza de Pescado (FISH CHOWDER)

Among gourmets the only base for bouillabaise, or any pis-catorial pretty is fish head soup, but don't mention the name if your guests haven't been around.

Discretion must be exercised in making the soup or stock to keep it delicate; the heads of any edible sea fish are excellent, but don't use them too many or too large.

1 medium or 2 small fish heads	4 tbs. cooking oil
2 onions, chopped	2 leeks
2 cloves garlic, chopped	6 medium potatoes
Whole pepper corns	2 medium carrots
2 bay leaves	2 cans tomato sauce
1 sprig each, thyme & marjoram	Salt and pepper

In two quarts of water put the fish to cook with one onion, one clove garlic, six pepper corns, bay leaves and the sprigs of thyme and marjoram. When it has cooked an hour and a half strain through a fine colander.

In the cooking oil sauté the other onion, garlic, leek, potatoes and carrots all chopped or sliced fine. When the onions are transparent add the tomato sauce and cook five minutes.

Add the fish stock to the vegetables, salt and pepper, and simmer for forty minutes.

Serve with Mexican rice, hot sauce and sliced limes.

Meat, Fowl and Eggs

Meat, Fowl
and Eggs

WHEN THE EARLY INDIANS of Mexico wanted red meat, they went after it with bow and arrow, javelin or snare. Deer, wild pigs and rabbits were known in most parts of the land, as well as armadillo, iguana and grasshoppers which are still popular tidbits. Toasted grasshoppers are now an export item from Mexico.

The Indians of South America domesticated the llama, vicuña and alpaca, but the only animal mentioned by Bernal Díaz and the other *conquistadores* that the Mexicans raised for food was a small dog.

Mexico is a land suited to stock, so shortly after the conquest thousands of square miles were dotted with cattle, pigs, sheep and goats. Today Mexican stock is generally good, and with government encouragement and supervision quality is upgrading constantly.

Along with the animals they brought, the Spaniards introduced methods of cookery. Meat dishes reflect old habits of dressing flesh before refrigeration was known. Meat was thinly sliced in long sheets then sprinkled with salt and herbs and smoked for storage. This treatment led to the habit of cutting meat with the grain. Evidently steaks cut across the grain were unknown to the Spaniards because the words we use today are foreign. *Filete* comes from the French *filet*, and *biftec*—(pronounced beeftake)—comes from our word beefsteak although it is used for either pork or beef, and the meat will more likely than not be cut along the grain.

Mexican and Spanish methods of grilling, spitting, frying, boiling, roasting, stewing and baking meats are similar to ours, but there are variations. The Mexican cook is a great hand to boil pork, and anything baked in the oven, *al horno*, is uncovered. An *asado*, or roast, is similar to our pot roast and is cooked in a *cazuela* on top of the stove. However, vegetables are seldom cooked with meat except in soup.

The word "barbecue" is a North American word and is thought to come from the Mexican word "*barbacoa*." The *barbacoa* is a stroke of genius that comes from pre-Conquest days and is almost identical with the luau in Hawaii.

To prepare *barbacoa* a large pit is dug and lined with lime stone or volcanic rock, and a blazing fire is maintained for five or six hours until the stones are almost red hot. The fire is allowed to die down, then the pit is partially filled with maguey stalks. A dressed goat, pig, sheep or part of a beef wrapped in leaves is laid on top. The pit is covered, and the meat cooks in the aromatic steam of the maguey juice.

Barbacoa is prepared in a tightly closed clay *olla* and dispensed in cafes and at all *fiestas*. On the Pacific Coast of Mexico, especially in Colima, the word "*tatemar*" was used anciently for pit cooking. Today the word has died out, and only one specialized pork dish retains the name "*tatemado*."

Agujas de Monterrey (BARBECUED GOAT RIBS)

The little goat occupies a big place in the affections of Mexico. Songs are written about him, and "The Little Goat" is danced at fiestas while a game called "Goat and Coyote" is played all over the Republic. However, our southern neighbors love the goat or kid most of all when he appears in the *olla* or on the coals.

Monterrey is the center for the *cabra* gourmet, and anyone who passes through town without savoring *agujas* has his trencherman's card lifted. To enjoy *agujas* at their taste-bud tickling tops catch a horse-drawn carriage, called a *calandria*, in the Plaza and drive out Hidalgo to Quinta Calderon. The half hour ride past flower filled yards and strolling señoritas will pique your appetite perfectly for a two o'clock *comida*.

In the spacious grounds of the Quinta is Café Tío where only beef and goat dishes are served. A soft voiced waiter in dinner jacket takes your order and allows you to carry your drink for a stroll out to the barbecue room where the meat spits over deep beds of mesquite coals.

When your ration is ready the waiter rolls it proudly to the table on a *parrilla*, or grill, with ardent coals almost kissing the *agujas*. Nothing is allowed to distract from the golden, barbecued ribs. Rolls and butter with red and green sauces stand mute on the far sides of the table, but no supporting roles are allowed.

When the leisurely meat course is finished, the *mozo* clears the table and bears in a steaming bowl of *frijoles a la charra*, cowgirl style beans, brewed from the *bayo gordo* bean. The *bayo gordo* or fat bay is only fat in size, actually it is light in the bowl and in the stomach.

This charming but unpretentious soup is made by sautéing a small amount of lean bacon with a clove of garlic and an onion and adding to the beans when they are boiling. A pinch of cumin and coriander is stirred in, and the beans are salted just before they are done.

After the guest finishes the *frijoles* and drinks a cup of cheering Mexican coffee he feels like tiptoeing out of the Uncle Cafe in reverence.

Albondigón a la Mexicana (MEXICAN MEAT LOAF)

Most Spanish words beginning with "al" come from the Arabic, so this exotic plate goes back at least to the time of the Moors. Classically it is raider's food; capture a ranch or hacienda and there are all the ingredients waiting to be potted. If you see a movie of the Mexican Revolution, particularly of Villa's Brigade of the North, watch the soldiers' women cooking over the camp fires; they are making *albondigón*.

Albondigón is a splendid dish to serve with a full scale Mexican meal or at a barbecue, because its exotic tang brings Chihuahua to your table. When you unwrap the savory roll, have all hands join in a few bars of "Cucaracha."

3 chorizos (optional)	2 tsps. chili powder
2 onions	Vinegar
1 lb. lean, ground beef	1 bay leaf
1 lb. lean sausage	Thyme
4 eggs	Marjoram
1 chicken breast	Oregano
1 cup pitted olives	1 lb. sliced tomatoes
3 green, pickled peppers	5 sliced avocados
Salt and pepper	

Skin chorizos and grind with onions; add to ground meat. Mix in eggs, chicken well chopped, olives and peppers seeded and finely chopped and season with salt, pepper and chili powder.

Mix thoroughly and wrap in thin cloth; roll out in the form of a cylinder and pin or sew the cloth together. Put in a pot with enough water to just cover the *albondigón* and add two cups of vinegar with a leaf each of bay, thyme, marjoram and oregano. The water should be boiling when the *albondigón* is dropped in, and it needs two hours' cooking. There are many variations in preparing *albondigón*; some *soldaderas* sauté the meat and onions first while others add a half cup of bread crumbs or corn meal as a binder.

Unwrap the *albondigón*, slice on a platter and garnish with tomatoes and avocados. Have side dishes of *salsa* and *frijoles refritos*. Ample for eight revelling raiders.

Asado de Lomo de Puerco con Hongos
(ROAST PORK LOIN WITH MUSHROOMS)

Puebla was occupied by the French for the entire four years of the Empire, and their culinary impact must have been felt, for Puebla is accepted as the city of good food.

This Mexican Stroganoff is a fine example of Puebla cookery; it is simple and restrained yet it is *distinguido*.

2 lbs. lean pork loin	2 cups tomato juice
1 cup mushrooms	Salt and pepper
1 tbs. cooking oil	1 tbs. corn starch
1 large onion, chopped	

Brown the meat and mushrooms until the pork is golden then add the onions and sauté until they are tender. Lift the meat out for a moment and stir in the tomato juice, so the sauce is uniform.

Put the meat back in the sauce, cover tightly and cook in the oven at 275° for an hour and a half. Now mix the corn starch with a little water, stir into the sauce and cook another fifteen minutes. Slice and serve with *sopa de arroz*, salad and hard rolls. Serves four.

Asado de Plátanos (STEAK WITH BANANAS)

In tropical America there are dozens of varieties of bananas ranging from tiny, almost white ones with a tangy taste to giant reds, called *machos*. The true cooking banana is a plantain and cannot be eaten raw.

Usually only one type of banana is sold in the United States, and it has been developed for its shipping qualities. To choose bananas for frying, pick the largest fruit possible, with firm flesh and skin as green as you can find.

2 lbs. round steak	1 tbs. cooking oil
Salt and pepper	2 tbs. sugar
1 chopped onion	4 cooking bananas
½ cup sherry & ½ cup water	

Fry the steak quickly over fast heat until both sides are well browned, salt and pepper, drop in the chopped onion and pour in the wine and water. Cover *tightly* and cook slowly until a fork passes easily through it.

In another pan heat the oil, sprinkle in the sugar and allow it to turn a golden color before adding the bananas cut in half lengthwise. When the bananas are well browned on both sides, they are ready.

Serve the meat in portions the size of small steaks, bathed in its own sauce with the bananas on the side. This makes four servings.

Asado de Ternero con Papas
(POT ROAST OF VEAL WITH POTATOES)

Ahuacatlán, which means place of the avocados, is a small, picturesque town in Nayarit state near a large government experimental cattle ranch. The village drowses all year to save its energies for the annual fiesta during the first week in October.

For two hilarious days the town swarms with barefoot Huichol Indians, entertainers and booted cattle ranchers wearing big hats and forty-five pistols. Young men spend the day in the church towers and swing the silvery toned bells in complete revolutions every fifteen minutes.

There is a carnival, native dances are swirled and a first class bull fight is staged, but the most important business of a fiesta is food, and Ahuacatlán takes a back seat to no other town in Mexico for its viands.

Café Capri stands on the main plaza and caters to ranchers and visitors; the local meat is excellent and their *asado de ternero* is the finest I tasted in the Republic.

1 ½ lbs. veal	3 tbs. butter
1 tbs. cooking oil	2 tbs. flour
2 carrots	1 cup broth
1 bunch *hierbas de olor*	1 wine glass sherry
1 leaf each bay, thyme,	6 medium potatoes
marjoram and oregano	2 tbs. chopped parsley
Salt and pepper	

Cut meat in 1 ½ inch pieces and brown in oil; cover with water and cook until tender with the carrots, *hierbas de olor*, salt and pepper.

Melt the butter and brown the flour, add 1 cup broth, wine, salt and pepper, and stir until smooth. Add meat to the sauce and cook until sauce thickens.

Serve on a platter surrounded by boiled, buttered potatoes sprinkled with parsley. Have plenty of refried beans and fresh *salsa*, shoot out the lights and start eating. Eight servings.

Barbacoa Tlaxcalteca (BARBACOA TLAXCALA STYLE)

Our word "barbecue" comes from *barbacoa*, but the two words no longer mean the same thing. A *barbacoa* must be cooked in a rock lined pit or in an airtight vessel. The primitive luaua and *barbacoa* are exactly alike except that the Hawaiians wrapped their fish or meat in banana leaves while the Aztecs and Tlaxcalans packed their food with maguey leaves or *pencas*.

The maguey—we call it century plant—holds in the meat's moisture and flavor and contributes more moisture and flavor. Today the meat is usually cooked in a tall clay olla and is frequently wrapped in heavy cloth.

2 lamb shoulders,
  each 2, 2½ lbs.
4 large bell peppers
3 cloves garlic
2 tsps. chili powder

¼ tsp. each clove, thyme,
  marjoram, cumin, cinnamon,
  pepper and oregano
2 bay leaves
Salt

Parboil the green peppers whole then seed and run garlic and peppers through food chopper; mix in all other ingredients except meat.

Now rub the meat on all sides with the dressing and wrap separately in three or four thicknesses of moist white cloth. Place in a dutch oven or heavy clay pot with good seal on top. If seal isn't sure, put a damp cloth over pot with lid on top.

Cook in oven at 275° for approximately three hours.

If you use a little water in the bottom of the pot, be sure to keep the meat above it on a rack.

With this feast serve green sauce and sliced avocados. For eight.

Biftecs con Chipotle
(BEEFSTEAKS PICKLED-PEPPER STYLE)

1 onion, sliced
3 tbs. cooking oil
2 lbs. round steak
1 no. 2½ can solid
  pack tomatoes

2 yellow chile peppers
  in vinegar
Salt

Sauté the onions and remove from pan; in same cooking oil and increased heat fry steaks on both sides quickly to seal.

Run tomatoes and seeded chiles through chopper, salt and pour over meat.

Cover vessel with tight sealing lid and simmer or bake at low heat for an hour and a half. Serves four.

Biftecs Molidos Adobados
(MOCK STEAK IN MARINADE)

1 lb. ground round
1 lb. pork sausage
  Salt & pepper
  Cooking oil

2 cloves garlic
½ cup tomato sauce
2 tbs. chili powder
  Pinch cumin

Sprinkle the meat with salt and pepper and mix thoroughly. Roll out into very thin steaks. Handle with care so as not to break and fry on both sides.

Squeeze the garlic through a press into tomato sauce and add chili powder and cumin. In the same oil where the meat was cooked pour the tomato *recaudo* and cook five minutes. Salt and add two table-spoons water.

In a casserole put a layer of steaks, cover with *recaudo*, build another layer of steaks and pour on rest of sauce. Cook in preheated 275° oven covered for thirty minutes.

Serve with onion rings and olives. Makes four portions.

Biftecs Enchilados (CHILI BEEFSTEAK)

Chili beefsteak is the answer to our pepper steak. Here is another good subject for the barbecue chef who wishes to add originality to his menu. It will also make a fine breakfast if you have a hard day ahead branding cattle or shoeing horses.

1 garlic clove	2 tbs. wine vinegar
2 tbs. chili powder	1 lb. steak

Crush the garlic and mix with the chili and vinegar to make a paste. Rub the steak with the chili *adobo* and let it stand three or four hours; fry in butter.

This is always served with plenty of fried potatoes, and the steak is not salted until you are ready to start eating. One steak per person.

Chile con Carne

In the United States chili con carne is predominantly a bean dish, but in Mexico *chile con carne* is a generous meat dish. Making a good *chile con carne* is like making a good marriage: you give the same narrow eyed scrutiny to finding the right type of bean that you would to choosing a wife. Look for sturdy character, consistent quality and recognized breeding.

It is my considered opinion as your marriage counsellor that the Mexican red bean should come first in your affection. Lacking that, choose the bay bean with third spot going to the pinto. Don't pick a wishy-washy helpmeet that will become puffed up, split at the seams when the heat is on or turn mushy in a crisis.

1 lb. dry beans	2 tsps. salt
2 lbs. lean stew beef in	1 tbs. corn starch or
¾ inch cubes	2 tbs. corn meal
2 bay leaves	1 ½ tsps. black pepper
2 large onions sliced	¼ tsp. each dried oregano, sage
1 clove garlic minced	and cumin, powdered
2 tbs. bacon fat or	1 tbs. chili powder or
vegetable oil	more to taste
5 raw tomatoes (I use	
2 cans tomato sauce)	

Have your woman pick the beans over for pebbles and put on to soak the night before. In the morning put the beans and meat on to cook and when they are boiling add bay leaves, onions and garlic.

When the beans are tender, heat up the frying pan, add oil, tomato sauce, salt, and the corn starch or corn meal and seasonings. Mix thoroughly and cook for five minutes then add to beans and simmer another hour. (Observe when the salt goes in; that's a thousand-year-old Aztec trick: salt hardens beans.) Serves eight.

Costillas de Puerco Asadas (BARBECUED PORK RIBS)

Every master of the backyard barbecue or cook-out knows that the savor of grilled ribs depends on a good marinade or basting sauce. The basic purpose of *adobo* is to preserve meat, but many *adobos* are excellent for basting. Try this simple baste for your next luau and you will be surprised at its cooperation.

For one pound of spare ribs mix an *adobo* of one half teaspoon black pepper, one quarter teaspoon cumin, one quarter teaspoon salt and three tablespoons vinegar. Rub the ribs with the *adobo* and let them stand an hour then barbecue them on the grill. Serve with *escabeche*.

Costillas de Ternero Adobado
(MARINATED VEAL RIBS)

For two pounds of ribs mix an *adobo* of two tablespoons peanut oil, one eighth teaspoon each of oregano, thyme, marjoram and pepper, one bay leaf, juice of half a lime or lemon and one teaspoon of vinegar.

Swab and let stand two hours and grill over a low fire. For four.

Estofado

Estofado is an ancient dish with the gentleness of age and the know-how of experience behind it. It likely started thousands of years ago in the Caucassus Mountains with mutton, salt, wild onion, garlic and mustard seed; gained bay leaves and black pepper in Turkey, picked up oregano and cumin from the Moors and took up with wine in Spain. In Mexico the *chile ancho* was dropped in and after the arrival of the first Manila galleon, curry was gingerly added.

Believe me, this is one of the most universal of dishes; everyone likes it. *Estofado* is not hot, and the herbs are as subdued as Montezuma was by Cortés. Serve it over or with rice and your guests will nod sagely and murmur: "Belly good."

3 lbs. lean raw pork, mutton or venison
3 tbs. cooking oil
2 large onions
2 cloves garlic
3 tsps. chili powder
2 bay leaves

1 tsp. each salt, curry, dry mustard
¼ tsp. each cumin, and pepper
1 cup sherry
2 drops barbecue smoke sauce (The last is my contribution to world gastronomy. Consider it optional)

Sauté meat, cut in two inch cubes, in clay or enamel roaster; when meat is golden add chopped onions and garlic and sauté to a soft yellow. Add all other ingredients, cover with a tight lid and cook two and a half to three hours in a 250° oven. Serves eight.

Estofado de Res Estilo Mexicano
(MEXICAN STYLE BEEF ESTOFADO)

The Mexican is about as independent and unreconstructed as anyone in the world. He speaks Spanish with an imagination and flair that few other Latin-Americans understand. The only French word left after Maximilian's four-year Empire is the *mariachi* orchestra. The French had the orchestras play at weddings and the musicians called themselves *marriage* orchestras.

They took the word "beefsteak" from us and glibly serve *biftecs* of pork, venison or beef. They know we like maple syrup on our *jat queques* (hot cakes), so they beamingly serve sorghum, honey or cane syrup and call it *ma-play*. As the rabbit in Lewis Carroll's story said: "Words mean what I want them to mean."

Observe the bland disregard of semantics in this beef *estofado*.

1 lb. lean beaf in cubes	2 cups broth
2 tsps. cooking oil	2 large sweet peppers
1 large onion	3 large tomatoes (or one
Salt and pepper	can tomato sauce)
1 bay leaf	6 medium potatoes
½ tsp. each thyme, marjoram and oregano	

Sauté the meat then add the onion and cook lightly, add salt, pepper, herbs and broth, cover and cook until meat is tender. Introduce the chopped peppers and tomatoes and cook another half hour before putting the quartered potatoes in.

Cook forty minutes until the liquid is thickened. Serves four.

Guisado de Res (BEEF AND VEGETABLES)

The Spanish dictionaries translate *guisado* as stew, but I have noted through bitter experience that dictionaries are put together by notorious non-cooks, and I can assure you that *guisado* is *guisado* is *guisado*.

This is a savory dish which somewhat resembles our cowboy potatoes.

2 lbs. flank steak	4 *chiles verdes* or one
¼ cup olive oil	bell pepper
5 carrots	2 slices raw ham
5 potatoes	1 bay leaf
1 large onion	1 cup soup stock
	Salt and pepper

The flank steak should be sliced very thin then cut into portions the size of a small steak.

Rub the bottom of a small but deep casserole with oil and cover with meat; over this put a layer of vegetables sliced thin, ham, some crushed bay leaf and more oil. Now lay in more meat and another layer of vegetables and continue until all ingredients are used.

Pour a cup of soup over the top, sprinkle with salt and pepper, cover and cook in the oven about forty minutes. More soup may be added if the *guisado* is drying out, but don't let it get soupy. Six.

Adobado con Hongos
(SPARERIBS WITH MUSHROOMS)

Every barbecue cook has his own method of preparing spareribs, and he usually searches industriously for new secrets to pique his pork.

Dress your pig in this sauce and your friends will acknowledge you as king of your alley. Always use a ceramic pot.

1½ lbs. pork spareribs	2 cans tomato sauce
Cooking oil	Salt
5 onions	½ tsp. ground oregano
8 cloves garlic	8 bell peppers
1½ lbs. fresh mushrooms	

Brown the ribs quickly on both sides.

Heat cooking oil in a casserole and slowly sauté the onions, well chopped, the whole garlic cloves and the mushrooms. Use small mushrooms whole but halve or quarter large ones.

Turn off the heat under the casserole, cover and let stand ten minutes. Remove the garlic cloves, reheat and add the meat, tomato sauce, salt, oregano and peppers cut in thin strips.

Cook slowly until the meat is done, about one hour at 250°. Four.

Lomo de Cerdo al Jerez
(BARBECUED PORK LOIN IN SHERRY)

In Northern Mexico where the mountains meet the desert is the four-hundred-year-old town of Parras of the Fountain. Parras is the oldest wine producing center in Mexico, and an annual fiesta is held each year in the late summer to celebrate the vintage. The porkers of Parras are fed the pressed grape hulls, and they are walking tons of Rabelaisian goodness.

To properly wed the pork loin with the daughter of the vine one should follow the hallowed practice of Parras. Invite the guests early and let them sit around a gallon *garrafa* of sherry in the kitchen. As the tantalizing odors escape, and the meat turns a golden brown everyone toasts the progress of the pig.

4 lbs. pork loin	2 tortillas
½ cup oil	1 can tomato sauce
2 cloves garlic	⅛ tsp. coriander
1 tbs. wine vinegar	2 tbs. chili powder
Salt and pepper	2 cups broth
¼ lb. almonds, chopped	1 cup sherry
1 sliced onion	

Rub the roast well with oil and put it in an open roaster. Cut slivers of garlic and hide them in the meat and sprinkle salt and pepper over the roast. Pour the rest of the oil and the vinegar over the roast and place in a 200° oven for an hour and a half, basting between drinks.

In a separate pan fry the blanched almonds in oil then fry the onion and finally the tortillas. Grind the almonds, onion and tortilla to form a paste, add the tomato sauce, coriander and chili powder and bring to a boil; season with salt and pepper and add broth and sherry.

Remove the loin from the roaster, but do not use the liquid. Slice the loin and add the slices to the sauce where it is cooked slowly for another hour. The sauce should thicken, but don't let it burn.

Sprinkle toasted sesame seed over the roast when it is ready and serve plenty of refried beans and hard rolls to dunk in the sauce.

Lomo de Puerco Adobado Estilo San Andrés Tuxtla

(SAN ANDRES TUXTLA STYLE LOIN OF PORK)

San Andrés Tuxtla lies in southern Vera Cruz state a few miles from the beautiful Lake Catemaco. Towering trees interlaced with flowering vines shade the white city while thousands of acres of sugar cane carpet the back country from the Gulf to the distant, lavender Sierra.

Porkers fortunate enough to grow up in this perennial garden spend their days strolling through groves of avocado, papaya and oranges and gratulating on the fallen fruit. To bring them to the complete fruition that nature intended, they are fattened on sugar cane and reach succulent maturity already sugar-cured.

They are also bursting with enzymes from the papaya, unction from the avocado and vitamins from the oranges, so it would seem redundant to pot roast them in orange juice. However over four hundred years of experience lie behind the local chefs, and the fact that they withhold the usual tomato sauce shows a rare confidence. They also wrap the meat in a toasted banana leaf, so if you wish to capture that kiss of the tropics mash a firm banana into the *adobo*.

2 lbs. pork loin	1 onion
2 slices boiled ham	1 clove garlic
4 slices lean bacon	Orange juice to cover
2 *chiles jalapeños*, or	meat in roaster
green chiles in vinegar	1 tbs. chili powder
Salt and pepper	1 firm banana (optional)

Cut the ham, bacon, and green chiles in narrow strips and peg the strips to the loin with toothpicks. (Be sure to remove before serving.) Sprinkle with salt and pepper.

Grind the onion and garlic and add to orange juice, then stir in chili powder. Pour this *adobo* over meat, cover tightly, and put in 350° oven for an hour and a half.

Slice and serve with *gazpacho* soup and *salsa*. A feast for four.

Mole de Olla Verde (GREEN POT STEW)

2 lbs. heart meat cubed	2 tsp. cooking oil
(trim all fat)	1 lb. potatoes
2 cloves garlic	1 lb. summer squash
2 lbs. green tomatoes	1 cup fresh or frozen peas
1 green sweet pepper	Pinch coriander
1 onion	Salt

Put the meat on to cook with chopped garlic and just enough water to cover; salt in half an hour.

Scald and peel tomatoes, seed and slice pepper, slice onions and put all through chopper. Cook in oil five minutes.

Add the meat with quartered potatoes, summer squash, peas, coriander and another sprinkle of salt. Mix and cook another half hour.

Serve with hot Mexican or French rolls and *frijoles refritos*. Eight.

Olla Totonaca (TOTONAC POTLUCK)

The Totonac Indians are found throughout the present state of Vera Cruz. The ones along the Gulf are fishermen and cultivators of tropical fruit while their brothers in the nine and ten thousand foot mountains, who were ancient hunters, herd stock and have small garden hanging to the sides of the steep highlands.

When the corn and beans are harvested and the fattest stock slaughtered thanksgiving is celebrated to Chicomoltzin, called Tajín in the low country, god of all foods.

Deer skin drums throb and *chirimías* whistle up the canyons in a call to the ceremonial dances. Aromatic wood fires send their smoke high over the ridges and the bubbling clay *ollas* waft tantalizing odors afar to tempt the timid old gods out of their hiding places.

The traveler on Highway 130 from Pachuca to Pozo Rico and

Papantla passes through the heartland of the old empire, and he is welcome to visit through the three-days of dancing, pulque drinking and *olla* feasting.

½ cup garbanzos	2 quarters of cabbage
½ cup white beans	3 small summer squash
1 lb. veal	3 chayotes (you can
1 lb. lamb	substitute potatoes)
½ lb. pork loin	3 onions
1 chicken	6 cloves of garlic
2 large slices of ham	¼ tsp. cumin
2 chorizos	¼ tsp. saffron
2 large, firm bananas	Salt and pepper
1 cup green beans	

Soak the garbanzos and beans all night. In the morning pour the beans and garbanzos in a deep clay pot with six quarts of water and drop in the cut up veal, lamb, pork and chicken. Cook for three hours then add the other ingredients. Leave the bananas in their skins and mix the saffron with water before adding it.

At the end of another hour step out back and pour a libation of stew on the ground for Chicomoltzin and give a war whoop to let the guests know fiesta has started.

Each guest should say *"Buen provecho"* before he starts dipping. Twelve servings.

Pierna de Carnero Escabechada
(MARINATED LEG OF LAMB)

The nuns of Santa Monica Convent in Puebla led a low-voiced leisurely life. Each sister had her regular routine in maintaining the buildings and grounds, and the cooks had it best of all.

Early in the morning they shopped the market for fresh meat, fruits and vegetables and returned to prepare them in the giant tile kitchen which was equipped with every size and type of copper and clay cooking utensil, while flat masonry stoves, stoked with charcoal, glowed invitingly through the day and much of the night. Outside the *cocina* was a large, sunny garden containing every herb known to the Mexican cuisine.

In such an atmosphere even the foods took on the casual air of the cooks and lingered in the kitchen for hours and days before appearing on the table. This leisurely leg of lamb is one of their greatest triumphs.

1 4-6 lb. leg of lamb	3 onions sliced
1 slice ham	½ tsp. each oregano & thyme
6 cloves garlic	1 cup olive oil
10 carrots sliced thin	2 cups wine vinegar
1 turnip quartered	Salt and pepper

With a sharp knife prick small holes in the meat and tuck in tiny pieces of ham and slices of garlic. Lay the meat in a dish just large enough to contain it and pour over it the *escabeche* made by mixing the vinegar, oil, herbs, vegetables, salt and pepper. Rub roast well and let it stand three days, turning it twice daily.

Pour off *escabeche*, wipe roast well and roast in open pan at 325° for three and a half hours. Cook the *escabeche* well, put through colander and serve with the meat as a sauce. Eight portions.

Puerco Tatemado (HERB PORK BARBECUE)

Colima is a peaceful, somnolent city which sits on a wide plain. The twin peaks of Colima volcano rear 8,000 feet above the plaza with one cone smoking and the other perpetually glistening with snow.

Tatemado is an Indian word and the dish is encountered only in the state of Colima, where it is the savory specialty of the capital. *Fruta en vinagre*, fruit in vinegar, which is used in preparing *tatemado* is a bit of Mexican whimsy, because it isn't fruit at all. It is made of vegetables—carrots, onions, potatoes, sweet peppers, cauliflower and green peas—pickled in vinegar for three days. A recipe is given in vegetable section.

Tatemado is always garnished with lettuce, onions and radishes and flanked with fried rice and pineapple. Another specialty of Colima, *tuba*, a slightly fermented drink made from palm blossoms, is also served with *tatemado*. However, anything you find in your cellar or refrigerator will fraternize with this genial dish.

2 lbs. lean pork (loin or chops are best)	Sprinkle cayenne
⅛ tsp. cumin, clove, cinnamon, allspice, thyme and coriander	5 cloves garlic, mashed
	½ cup *fruta en vinagre* (pickled onions may be substituted)
½ tsp. chili powder	½ cup vinegar
Salt and pepper	2 pimientos cut in thin strips

Mix spices and garlic and add enough water to make a thin paste. Cut the pork in one inch slices and brown. Swab the meat with this sauce and pour remainder over the top. Add pickled vegetables, cover and cook for an hour at 275°.

Uncover, pour in vinegar, stir and cook uncovered another 15 minutes or until thoroughly done. Put pimientos over *tatemado* at time of serving. Serves six.

Ropa Vieja (GYPSY STEW)

The gypsies have been wandering Mexico since the Conquest. As a matter of fact the original rolls frequently list a man as *un gitano*, a gypsy. Today few *fiestas* are complete without the colorful itinerants who sell herbs, swap horses, perform swirling dances to attract a crowd and tell fortunes.

Instead of the old time horse-drawn, covered wains that moved slowly over dusty roads, the gypsies travel in house trucks and carry their plunder in fast moving trailers. However they still camp on the outskirts of cities and dance around the campfire while the *olla* of *ropa vieja*—which means literally "old clothes"— bubbles merrily.

The classic way to cook this stew is in a clay *olla* with a cloth tied on top and a *cazuela* full of water over the cloth to contain every wisp of steam. However if you haven't been able to raid the countryside lately for such cooking ware, use any ceramic pot with a heavy, tight-fitting lid.

1 ½ lbs. lean stew beef or veal	½ cup cooking oil
5 tomatoes	2 cloves of garlic
2 onions	1 tbs. vinegar
1 sprig parsley	2 bay leaves
1 ½ pints soup stock	4 potatoes
Salt and pepper	3 bell peppers

Cut the meat in small pieces and put on to boil with chopped tomatoes, sliced onions, parsley, oil, chopped garlic, vinegar, bay leaves, soup stock, salt and pepper.

Cook slowly, moving the pot now and then to prevent sticking. When the meat is done add the quartered potatoes and the pepper cut in thin strips and sautéed.

Serve hot with rolls and *salsa verde*. Four servings.

Ternera en Nogada (ALMOND VEAL)

3 lbs. veal stew meat	3 tbs. butter
4 cloves garlic	½ cup ground walnuts
2 medium onions	1 large can evaporated milk
Salt and pepper	4 tbs. toasted and ground
⅛ tsp. thyme	almonds

Have the veal in one or two large pieces and put on to boil in a quart and a half of water with finely chopped garlic and one onion, salt, pepper and thyme. Cook over slow heat for one hour.

Remove from heat, cool and cut meat in thin slices. Save broth.

Melt the butter and sauté the other onion, chopped fine. Mix in the ground walnuts, the evaporated milk, salt pepper and the broth in which meat was cooked.

Drop in the sliced meat and continue to cook very slowly for half an hour.

When serving sprinkle ground almonds over each dish.

This recipe can also be used for left-over veal.

Broth may be thickened with 2 tablespoons cornstarch or flour, but south of the border, they like it thin. Serves six.

Gallina a la Mexicana (MEXICAN STYLE CHICKEN)

Chicken is a favorite the world over, but in Mexico *gallina* is worshipped, generally from afar. Chicken is sold at the markets and served in homes and restaurants, but in the humble dwellings of perhaps a third of the people it is never known. Their only acquaintance with the succulent bird comes at the annual fiesta.

High in the mountains of Puebla near the Hidalgo state line is the beautiful town of Huauchinango which holds a fiesta of the flowers in February. For two days floats and displays of domestic and wild flowers are paraded, topped off with hundreds of exotic orchids gathered in the forests.

From the wild woods also come hundreds of Indians and peons slipping silently along barefoot or in the leather thonged sandals they call *guaraches*. During the two day celebration they watch beauty paraded, go to Mass, crawl the length of the church on their knees and sleep on the ground wrapped in their *serapes*. In the morning the father grubs up a few centavos to buy himself and family tortillas with a dip of beans to stay their cold and hunger, and during the day they stand unmoving for hours and chew a piece of sugar cane.

But once during the fiesta each family has its glorious fling. Somehow during the year of poverty and toil the father has saved a small handful of tattered peso bills, and they all have their fill of *gallina a la Mexicana*.

They sit at a table in an open front restaurant, the father proudly wearing his hat, the mother holding her baby, and the children dangling their bare feet from the unaccustomed height of a chair. There is no thought of half portions or feeding the children from the parents' plates; each person has a full *comida*.

And for the only time of their stay, their inscrutable eyes light with joy and hope when they see the waitress approaching with their steaming bowls of *gallina*.

1 large stewing hen	1 cup chopped ham
1 bay leaf	½ cup pitted, green olives
2 chopped onions	2 tbs. capers (try green
3 cloves garlic	nasturtium seeds)
2 cans tomato sauce	1 tbs. ground almonds
2 tsps. chili powder	½ cup raisins, soaked
2 hard cooked egg yolks,	½ tsp. each thyme, oregano,
chopped	marjoram
1 cup rum or dry sherry	Salt and pepper

Cook the disjointed chicken in just enough water to cover with salt and a bay leaf.

Sauté the onion and garlic in a tablespoon of oil, then add all the other ingredients with a cup of chicken broth. Simmer a few minutes.

Put the chicken in a pot and cover with the *recaudo*; if there is a shortage of the sauce stir in more broth. Cover and allow to amalgamate the flavor for an hour over very low heat. Serves four.

Guajolote con Mole Poblano
(TURKEY WITH MOLE SAUCE)

Over two hundred years ago during Mexico's colonial period there were four convents in Puebla: Santa Rosa, Santa Monica, Santa Teresa and Santa Clara. Each convent had a large, tiled kitchen, several sisters who were master cooks and a reputation for excellent food.

One day the viceroy of Mexico arrived in pomp and splendor to visit the Bishop of Puebla, and the sisters vied with each other to furnish the most delectable dishes to the dignitaries. The *maestra* of Santa Rosa's kitchen, Sor Andrea de la Asunción, decided that something far-fetched would have to be done to pull ahead of such a distinguished company of cooks, so she took a simple old Indian dish called *mole* and tossed in all the goodies in the *cocina*.

The result was a smash hit which has become a national favorite, *mole poblano*. Convents in Mexico were all closed by the Reform Laws of 1857, and today Santa Rosa is a working class rooming house. However the tiled kitchen still stands proud and aloof, and if the visitor finds the little hunchbacked woman with the ring of keys, she will unlock the *cocina*.

Puebla is known as the city of tile and the center of fine food, and the kitchen of Santa Rosa combined both. The polychrome tile still glistens clean, and the copper and clay *ollas* and *cazuelas* stand or hang in their appointed places.

The last time I visited Santa Rosa the little caretaker asked: "Would the Señor like the Sisters' cooking *recetas*?"

Would I? So for twice the price of a full size cook book I bought a poorly printed pamphlet of less than fifty pages. However it was worth the full price, for it contained Sor Andrea's original recipe.

1 roasting turkey, cooked	1 tsp. cinnamon
2 lbs. *chile mulato*	½ tsp. cloves
2½ lbs. *chile pasilla*	½ tsp. pepper
2½ lbs. *chile ancho*	1 hard roll crumbled and
1 lb. tomatoes	fried brown
2½ lbs. almonds	1 fried tortilla
½ lb. raisins	Broth from turkey
⅓ lb. sesame seed, toasted	Salt to taste
6 cloves garlic	1 tbs. sugar
Chile seeds to taste	4 small squares of baking
1 tbs. anise	chocolate

The chiles are washed, seeded and disveined. As most of the heat in chile peppers lies in the seeds enough seeds are left in to give the desired piquancy. Now fry the chiles, tomatoes, almonds, raisins, seeds and garlic then put them through the grinder (unless you have a stone molcajete).

Drop the ground ingredients into a hot *cazuela* and add spices and ground bread and tortilla. Pour in just enough soup stock so the *mole* cooks without sticking then add the salt, sugar and ground chocolate. Stir slowly until it thickens as you would any gravy. Serve over hot turkey.

I have taken no liberties with this recipe. You can buy the chiles at Mexican or specialty stores. You can also buy canned *mole*.

Our large bell or sweet pepper is almost the same as *chile mulato*, the *pasilla* is the long, thin Anaheim chile, and three tablespoons of chili powder meets the *chile ancho* requirement. Serves six.

Guajolote Mexicano (MEXICAN TURKEY)

Turkey is the royal feast of Mexico. The *guajolote* is often called "Moctezuma's Bird," and although the masses can't afford this delicacy, and frequently never taste it in their lifetime, they still revere it from afar. Other thousands eat turkey *mole* once a year at a religious fiesta or wedding.

An Englishman, H. B. C. Pollard, observed in 1913: "As a crowning delight, *mole de guajolote* was served. For this dish, turkey and chili sauce, a Mexican will commit murder. I am almost inclined to think it worth while, for the combination is delightful..."

In Mexico the turkey is still the domesticated wild bird that he was when the Spaniard came. He is a slight, athletic, self-sustaining creature that ranges in color from pure white and yellow to black.

The country is full of turkeylore, but Colima has one of the most interesting customs in preparing the *guajolote* for his greatest hour. He is fed tequila until he passes out, not for humanitarian reasons, but to tenderize the meat.

I have seen the ritual many times and it always goes the same. The turkey struggles while the first tablespoon is poured down his throat; then he gets a speculative look and holds still for the second draught ten minutes later. He is utter co-operation for the third swallow, and that is generally all it takes. Ten or fifteen minutes later he tries to take a step and falls on his face; that is the signal for the glorious sacrifice.

One ritual that does not vary in all of Mexico is the method of cooking the *guajolote*. The bird is boiled until it is almost tender then put in the oven in an open roaster and browned. As high heat is used the fowl is turned two or three times and basted; the result is boiled meat with a brown cover hard as pork rind.

After this treatment, it speaks highly indeed for the *mole* that raises the dish to such legendary heights.

Clemole

Clemole is a festival dish that is served in villages which retain their communal set up. In the first few days of January the townspeople come to the headman's house to pay the few cents that is their share for the fireworks in the Christmas fiesta. The mayor has a large olla of *clemole* simmering all day long, and each client eats a leisurely bowlful and visits before discharging his debt.

1 chicken	3 tbs. peeled squash seed
1 lb. pork loin	3 tbs. sesame seed toasted
2 tbs. oil	1 onion chopped fine
¼ lb. *longaniza* or smoked sausage	2 cloves garlic chopped (if chorizo is not used)
3 chorizos—optional	2 pimientos sliced
¼ cup almonds	Salt and pepper
¼ cup peanuts	Dash cayenne

Cut the chicken and loin into serving size chunks and boil until almost done.

In two tablespoons olive or peanut oil fry the *longaniza* and *chorizo*; when they are done remove and lightly fry the unblanched almonds, peanuts and squash seed. Remove and grind the nuts, seeds and toasted sesame seeds and dissolve in a quart of broth from the meat.

In the same oil brown the pieces of chicken and chunks of loin. Now add all other ingredients and the meat broth; cook until the sauce thickens and serve very hot.

If you want the full pious flavor, this dish is eaten with nothing but a folded tortilla. Serves six.

Chileatole Tezuiteco
(CHICKEN AND DUMPLINGS, TEZUITLAN)

Many of Mexico's finest dishes were originally ritual foods partaken of only at festivals of thanks to their many gods for a specific harvest. Even today at the annual *fiesta* for the patron saint of every village and church in the country there is a featured food. This may be a local maturing fruit or vegetable as the cactus pears of Zapopan, a wild creature as the wild duck *fiesta* at Lake Patzcuaro, or a prepared pot.

When the young corn is in the roasting ear stage the fresh young goddess, Xilonen (Shelonen) is thanked, but the "lady of the old skirt" who is patroness of dry maize is also remembered. *Chileatole* memorializes both ladies in a fitting manner. Be pleased to pay meet reverence when approaching this offering to the gods.

1 3 lb. chicken	⅓ cup cornmeal
2 lbs. pork ribs, country style	1 tsp. cornstarch
½ tsp. ground marjoram	2 eggs
Salt and pepper	⅓ tsp. bacon fat
3 sliced zucchini	⅛ tsp. thyme
8 ears sweet corn	½ tsp. soda
Bolitas or Corn Dumplings	

Cut the chicken in fairly small portions, add the pork ribs, marjoram and enough water to cover. Salt and pepper and bring to boil. When the meat is almost done add the zucchini and the corn in the following manner. Cut the corn from three ears, grind and put through colander; cut the kernels from two ears and put them in whole; cut three ears into wheels about a quarter inch thick and drop in.

To make corn dumplings mix cornmeal, cornstarch, eggs, bacon fat, soda and thyme. Make *bolitas* the size of walnuts and let them set half an hour. After the corn has been added let the soup come to a boil once more and drop in *bolitas*.

Corn *masa* is used in Mexico to make the *bolitas*, and I have worked up this substitute recipe with cornmeal. Feel free to vary it further. Prepared biscuit flour may be used for cornstarch. Serves eight.

Pollitos en Vino Tinto (FRYERS IN RED WINE)

Pollitos en Vino Tinto is the ideal serving for the host who wants an undeniably Mexican dinner that is not too exotic for northern tastes. The pot is unspiced yet strangely pleasing.

2 plump fryers	Salt and pepper
½ cup olive oil	3 slices bacon
½ cup vinegar	1 bunch green onions
1 large onion chopped	2 crisp carrots
2 cloves garlic	2 cans tomato sauce
1 bunch *hierbas de olor*	½ bottle dry red wine
(1 leaf each bay, thyme, marjoram & oregano)	

Cut the chickens up for frying and marinate for 24 hours in oil, vinegar, onion, garlic, herbs, salt and pepper.

Next day fry the bacon in a ceramic pot, remove most of the grease and lightly sauté the chopped green onions and chopped carrots; add the tomato sauce and cook for five minutes.

Now add the chicken with all the marinade, pour in the wine and cook until the chicken is thoroughly tender but not shredded.

Have a pitcher of Margaritas to marinate the guests.

Serve garlic French bread, *sopa de arroz* and red *salsa* with the chicken. Four helpings with seconds.

Pollo con Especias (SPICED CHICKEN)

For the Rakehell who likes his grog strong, his food zesty and his women full-bodied this pot is dedicated. There is little heat but distinct character and keen savor.

1 large, plump and tender chicken	⅛ tsp. clove
3 tbs. cooking oil	1 tbs. sesame seed
Salt and pepper	1 cup tomato sauce
2 cloves garlic	1 pinch saffron or savory
1 slice toasted bread, ground	1 tbs. vinegar
½ tsp. cinnamon	½ cup sherry

Cut the chicken in serving pieces, rub well with oil, salt and pepper and place in the broiler uncovered to brown.

Sauté the garlic in oil then add the ground toast, spices, and sesame seed. Pour in the tomato sauce, stir thoroughly and cook five minutes. Add the saffron, vinegar and wine.

When the chicken is pleasantly brown, pour the sauce over it, cover and bake until the chicken is tender, tender—about an hour at 275°. Serves four.

Pollo con Naranjas (CHICKEN WITH ORANGE)

El Naranjo Motel is a dreamer's dream. It sits beside the deep blue Naranjo River on Highway 80, twenty miles west of Antiguo Morelos.

The white cottages are shaded by a grove of mangoes, golden papayas flank the gurgling irrigation canal and banana trees, bowed by heavy fruit stalks, cover the river slope.

Rhode Island Red chickens lead lives of quiet decorum in their modern chicken run on the edge of a large orange grove and achieve their greatest hours in *Pollo con Naranjas*. Blessed is he who has sat on the bougainvillea shaded veranda overlooking the cascading river and considered this feast.

1 large, tender chicken	1 cup water
Salt and pepper	Pinch saffron
⅛ tsp. cinnamon	2 tbs. seedless raisins
⅛ tsp. clove	20 almonds
3 tbs. cooking oil	1 tbs. capers
2 cloves garlic	3 Valencia oranges, peeled
1 onion, chopped	and sliced
Juice of 3 oranges	

Cut the chicken in pieces, salt, sprinkle with condiments, and brown quickly in the oil.

When the fowl first starts to turn golden add the garlic, whole, and the chopped onion. When the meat is a uniform brown but not crusted, add the juice of three oranges, water, saffron, raisins, almonds, and capers.

Cover quietly, as these well-bred chickens aren't used to sudden noises, and as Samuel the cook always directed, "cook very suavely until the little chicken is tender."

Remove the garlic cloves, serve and adorn with peeled, sliced orange. Unobtrusively furnish side dishes of *sopa de arroz* and glasses of chilled, dry white wine. Serve to four dreamers.

Pollo Tapado (CHICKEN FIESTA)

Here is a tropical version of Thanksgiving chicken. The proud, plump roaster is escorted by the fruits of a fat harvest.

1 large roasting chicken, cut up	2 solid pears
Cooking oil	2 solid bananas
1 large onion	2 slices pineapple
3 large tomatoes	Medium can peas or
1 lb. small summer squash	package frozen
or zucchini	Salt and pepper

Fry the chicken lightly in cooking oil until it is brown on both sides but not done.

In a small but deep casserole place a layer of chicken then cover with fruit and vegetables. Slice the onion, tomatoes, squash and pears; slice the bananas crosswise leaving the skin on.

Rub everything lightly with oil; salt and pepper.

Now build another layer of chicken and another topping of fruit and vegetables. Season and cover the vessel.

Cook approximately one and one-half hours at 275° in a preheated oven. Six servings.

Huevos Tuidy (TWEEDY STYLE EGGS)

In 1900 Mrs. Alec Tweedy, a British authoress, spent six months travelling over Mexico as a guest of the Republic. Later she published *Mexico as I Saw It*. Quite a bit of fuss was made over her visit. At one time the natives displayed a large flower sign that read; "Welcome Mrs. Fweedy."

In Alvarado while she and her party awaited the paddle wheel steamer that was to take them up the vast Papaloapan River, the local *maestro de cocina* designed and served this delicately blended dish.

10 hard cooked eggs	½ cup thick cream
3 small fillets of snook or other ocean fish, cooked	1 tsp. grated onion
1 cup mayonnaise	
1 tsp. lime juice	1 can pimientos, sliced thin
Salt and pepper	

Shred the fish as fine as possible and add the lime, salt, pepper, cream and onion. Mix thoroughly into a thick paste.

Split the eggs lengthwise and remove the yolks then stuff with paste. Spoon mayonnaise over each egg and arrange strips of pimiento on top in form of flowers.

Chill slightly and serve.

Huevos Revueltos con Plátanos
(BANANA SCRAMBLE)

5 firm almost green bananas	Cooking oil
5 eggs	Salt

Cut the bananas in small pieces and brown them; mix in the eggs and scramble. Serves four.

Huevos en Reloj (EGG CLOCK SALAD)

1 lb. medium sized potatoes	2 tbs. prepared mustard
Vinegar and oil to taste	Salt and pepper
3 tbs. chopped parsley	1 head lettuce
6 hard cooked eggs	1 can pimientos
1 can deviled ham	

Either make a Mexican potato salad of thinly sliced, boiled potatoes, chopped parsley, oil and vinegar—or make your own favorite variety.

Cut the eggs in half lengthwise and remove the yolks. Chop the yolks fine with a fork and mix with the deviled ham, mustard, oil and vinegar to a firm paste. Stuff the eggs and keep the leftover paste.

Cover the bottom of a large glass platter, preferably round, with lettuce. The Mexicans always slice lettuce rather than serving in leaves as we do. Serve the potato salad over the lettuce.

Now comes the chef's turn to show his artistry. With the leftover egg stuffing make a circle over the potato salad. Around the circle arrange the egg halves uniformly. On each egg make a Roman numeral with small slices of pimiento. When you finish you should have the hours I, II, III up to XII around the circle.

Make the hour hand and minute hand of other strips of pimiento, with a tiny wheel around the center of the clock.

Huevos Rancheros (RANCH STYLE EGGS)

In the high country of Central Mexico, winter mornings are always nippy. The men lean against walls or hunker down in sunny corners with their serapes over their heads and puff slowly on cigarettes. Some of the women unroll their wares for a day's selling in the market while others walk along silently shopping for fruit and vegetables. Each one has a *reboza* wrapped around her head and shoulders with only a tiny opening left for her breath to leave a vapor trail.

That is the kind of morning that begs for, nay it demands, a breakfast of *huevos rancheros* fortified with a hot cup of coffee with milk, chocolate, *atole* or *champurrado*.

6 tortillas	2 small, piquant green chiles
Oil for frying	or 2 tbs. bell pepper chopped
1 onion, chopped	with 2 drops Tabasco sauce
1 clove garlic, minced	2 cups tomato sauce
	6 eggs

Fry tortillas quickly but don't let them get hard or crisp. Sauté the onion, garlic, and chilis, add tomato sauce and cook five minutes. Fry the eggs, sunny side up, put each one on a tortilla, pour tomato sauce over the top and serve. Sliced avocado and cheese adds a nice fillip.

Huevos a la Nieve (EGGS IN THE SNOW)

This is a superb *antojito* to serve with beer while watching a football game on TV; it is equally majestic served as an *entremés* to open the meal.

6 hard cooked eggs	½ onion, chopped
1 small can deviled ham	1 cup cream, whipped
1 tbs. chopped parsley	Parmesan cheese
1 tbs. prepared mustard	Salt

Cut the eggs in half and remove the yolks. Mix ham with egg yolks, onion, parsley and mustard. Lightly salt the mix and stuff the egg whites.

Put the halves together, lay all the eggs on a platter, cover with whipped cream, salt lightly and sprinkle with Parmesan cheese.

Tortilla con Mermelada (OMELETTE WITH JAM)

When you get tired of the same old guests and the same old recipes, better you change recipes and keep your friends. Serve this and your guests will have something different to talk about.

6 eggs	2 tbs. orange marmalade
1 jigger curaçao	Salt and nutmeg
2 tbs. butter	Brown sugar

Beat the eggs with salt and curaçao until they are uniform and cook slowly in butter until a firm omelette is formed.

Spread the omelette with marmalade, double over and sprinkle with brown sugar and a trifle of nutmeg.

Place under top heat a few seconds to brown, then serve.

Serve only black coffee with the tortilla. Four portions.

Huevos de los Reyes
(EGGS FOR THE KING AND QUEEN)

6 hard cooked eggs	3 tbs. finely chopped black olives
1 can cream of mushroom soup	1 tbs. capers
1 cup evaporated milk	1 tbs. butter
½ can pimientos, chopped	Parsley
6 slices toasted bread	Salt and pepper

Mix the soup and milk with a beater then add pimientos, olives, capers, salt and pepper. Heat slowly to boiling.

Butter the hot toast and place eggs, sliced in half lengthwise, on top of the toast. Pour the hot sauce over the eggs and garnish with parsley.

Vegetables, Salads, Herbs and Sauces

Vegetables, Salads, Herbs and Sauces

In the united states we are constantly bombarded by lectures from angular spinsters or earnest plump men on the necessity of eating plenty of vegetables if we care to remain healthy, energetic, regular and fertile. Between bites of potatoes and gravy, parents nag their children to force down their spinach, rutabaga or curly endive.

On the other hand the Mexican is completely uninvolved emotionally about *legumbres*. If a bunch of spinach shows up, it is chopped and sprinkled in the bean pot, because Juan dearly loves to see greenery floating on his soup. If a potato or two comes her way, Juana tosses them in the meat *olla;* it wouldn't occur to her to lay them out, pale and naked, on a separate plate.

There are few vegetables served solo in the Mexican *cocina;* they end up in a *guisado, adobado* or *estofado*, or are incorporated in that unique dish, *budín*. A Mexican pudding, like the English pie, is usually made of meat or vegetables, and it is tasty and tempting.

The Mexican philosophy is simple: if it's worth eating, it's worth dressing up to taste good.

There are two widespread and interesting schools of superstition concerning the herbs and vegetables of Mexico; one school is nurtured in the United States, the other in Mexico.

American writers, guides, casual acquaintances and even doctors who have never seen the Republic tell prospective visitors, with all the assurance of a Nahuatl witch doctor, that Mexicans

79

use "night soil" on their gardens and that therefore the vegetables should not be eaten under any circumstances.

I lived in China for 18 months and saw every phase of the dipping and exploitation of human excrement, euphemistically called "night soil," as a fertilizer. I have lived a considerably longer time in Latin America, and I can categorically state that not only is "night soil" never employed, but, outside of a few government experimental farms, fertilizer of any kind is seldom used. A well scrubbed vegetable is as safe in Mexico as it is in Arkansas.

Mexican beliefs are far more colorful. *Curanderos*, or herb doctors, flourish in every village of Mexico. They can be found in the markets where they sell every type of herb, seed and dried reptile, and prescribe for your every symptom. The yellow-flowered weed that we call dog fennel is used to make the famous *té de Manzanilla*. Thousands of gallons are drunk every day in Mexico to fend off all ills known to man.

In *Hamlet*, Ophelia mentions "rosemary for remembrance," but herbs are far more versatile in Mexico. Thyme, rosemary and oregano are specifics for stomach upset, toothache and menstrual trouble. Anise soothes rheumatism; garlic cleanses one of cancer; the smoke from burning pepper tree leaves chases the spirits that cause fevers; guava leaf tea heartens the intestines; onions guard against venereal disease and the tomato cures infections.

Dietetic research has found that the tropical *papaya* is the greatest natural producer of digestive enzymes, all the chile peppers are phenomenal sources of Vitamins A and C and are also marvelous digestants. The tea from lemon leaves is almost magical in its properties.

When one assesses all of this profound learning, he can hardly believe how much he is getting in one Mexican plate of vegetables and herbs.

Frijoles Carmelita (BEANS CARMELITA)

Mexico is the home of the bean and the Mecca of bean cookery. Warmed over beans can be as untempting as cold fried potatoes, but this creation is as fresh and sparkling as Carmelita in a new green and red blouse.

1 tbs. chopped onion	2 cups cooked chicken, chopped
1 sweet pepper, chopped	1 can tomatoes
1 clove garlic, chopped fine	2 tsps. chili powder, optional
Cooking oil	Salt
2 cups cooked beans	

Sauté the onion, pepper and garlic in cooking oil until onion is tender and golden. Add the other ingredients and simmer for an hour and a half. Serves six.

Arroz con Frijoles (BAKED RICE AND BEANS)

When a customer is undecided over food or drink in Mexico the vendor generously asks, "Would you like to prove it?" and gives him a sample.

Rice and beans appears so redundant to the North American imagination that the only way to open the door on a new taste sensation is to "prove" it.

3 cups cooked rice	1/5 lb. gruyere cheese, sliced thin
3 cups refried beans	½ pt. fresh cream
2 green peppers in	2 tbs. butter
narrow slices	Salt and pepper

In an open baking dish rubbed with butter, spoon a layer of rice, then cover with a layer of beans. Add a dollop of cream and sliced peppers and cheese. Continue building until the ingredients are used. Spot a few pats of butter on top and bake at 360° until food is heated uniformly. Serves six.

Frijoles Blancos con Perlas de Cebada (WHITE BEANS AND PEARL BARLEY)

This isn't the world's fanciest or most esoteric recipe; it's just about the world's best white bean creation.

1 lb. navy beans	1 small onion, chopped
½ cup pearl barley	1 bay leaf
1 small ham butt	Salt and pepper
1 clove garlic, chopped	

Don't bother to soak navy beans. Put them on to cook with all ingredients except the salt. At the end of two hours remove the bay leaf and add salt. Simmer for three more hours. Serves eight.

Ejotes con Pimientos
(GREEN BEANS WITH SWEET PEPPERS)

1 lb. green beans	3 bell peppers
1 tbs. chopped onion	1 tbs. chopped parsley
2 tbs. cooking oil	Salt and pepper

French cut the beans in long, thin strips and cook in a minimum of salted water. Drain.

Sauté the onion in oil until transparent but unbrowned; add the beans, peppers cut in long, thin slices and parsley. Continue cooking, covered, over slow heat until peppers are tender—perhaps five minutes. Add a tiny bit of the bean broth, salt and pepper and serve. Garnish each plate with sliced, hard-cooked eggs. Serves four.

Lentejas con Frutas (LENTILS WITH FRUIT)

Lentils may well be the first seed men learned to cook. They have lived with man and his whims thousands of years, but seldom have they lived with the flair they do in this tropical *mezclado*.

Here is Mexican imagination in its highest, keening flight.

1 lb. lentils	½ lb. cooked sweet potatoes
1 tbs. chopped onion	1 large banana, as green and
1 clove garlic	firm as possible
2 tbs. cooking oil	2 firm pears
2 cans tomato sauce	Salt and pepper
2 slices pineapple	

Wash lentils well and soak over night. Cook in plenty of water and be sure lentils are soupy when they finish boiling.

Make *recaudo* by sautéing onions and garlic; then add tomato sauce. Cook five minutes and add lentils with liquid. Add the pineapple in chunks, and the sliced sweet potatoes, bananas and pears which are peeled, cored and sliced.

When the pears are tender the *potage* is ready.

If this is what Essau sold out for, he got a good bargain. For eight.

Budín de Elote (SWEET CORN PUDDING)

This pudding serves a different purpose in a Mexican comida than it would in a meal in the United States. *Budín* is served as the second course, called the *pasta*, and whets one's appetite for the main courses to come.

4 cups fresh sweet corn, cut from cob or canned	6 eggs
½ cup sugar	3 tbs. seedless raisins
	Butter and salt

Salt the fresh corn and cook in a small amount of milk; drain and grind in food chopper. Mix the corn and sugar and heat slowly in a casserole with three tablespoons of melted butter; stir often to keep from burning until it is dry.

Turn the corn into a bowl and mix in the well beaten eggs and raisins. Spoon into a muffin tin, sprinkle with bread crumbs and bake fifteen minutes at 300°.

Set the tin in cold water for a minute and the pudding will come out without tearing.

Serve in saucers and sprinkle with sugar and cinnamon. For six.

Calabacitas a la Mexicana
(MEXICAN SUMMER SQUASH)

Centuries ago the squash was developed in Mexico from a wild gourd, and today gourds, squash and summer squash are all *calabazas*. The word ended up in this country as calabash.

This tasty dish of stewed vegetables is loaded with vitamins and low in calories.

½ lb. lean pork meat	2 lbs. summer squash
3 tbs. cooking oil	2 bell peppers, sliced
2 medium potatoes	2 ears fresh corn
1 clove garlic	Salt and pepper
½ onion chopped	Parmesan cheese

Cut the meat in thin strips and sauté in cooking oil until it is light brown. Add the tomatoes, onion and garlic all finely chopped. After five minutes of cooking drop in thinly sliced squash and bell peppers. Cut the kernels of corn from one ear and cut the other ear into thin wheels.

Add the corn, salt and pepper and cook about twenty minutes in its own juice, adding no water.

Serve and sprinkle with Parmesan cheese. Six servings.

Calabacitas con Crema
(SUMMER SQUASH IN CREAM)

Here is a dish delicate enough for the palate of an epicure or the stomach of an invalid.

1 lb. young, tender summer squash	1 pt. fresh cream
4 bell peppers	1 tbs. butter
1 small onion	Salt and pepper

Slice the summer squash and peppers as thinly as possible and chop the onion fine. Melt the butter in a ceramic vessel, pour in the vegetables and cook until tender without a drop of water.

Add the cream, stir and serve. As an added fillip it is interesting to add a tablespoon of Parmesan or Gruyere cheese, powdered. For four.

Calabacitas Rellenas
(STUFFED SUMMER SQUASH OR ZUCCHINI)

2 lbs. tender summer squash or zucchini	½ lb. ground lean pork
1 small onion finely chopped	2 tomatoes chopped
1 tbs. butter	2 tbs. finely chopped parsley
½ lb. ground lean beef	Salt and pepper
	1 egg

Wash summer squash, trim both ends and cook in boiling, salted water. When tender, pour off water and cool. Split the squash lengthwise and spoon out the meat.

Sauté the onion in butter lightly, then add the crumbled meat and cook gently for ten minutes. Mix in the tomatoes, parsley, salt and pepper, and chopped summer squash. Allow to cook and season another fifteen minutes. Beat in the egg quickly and thoroughly and stuff the squash shells.

Put the stuffed squash in an open, buttered baking dish, place a small piece of butter on each squash and leave in a 300° oven just long enough to brown lightly. Choose the zucchini for eight servings.

Chícharos a la Norteña
(GREEN PEAS NORTHERN MEXICO STYLE)

In the state of Chihuahua a few miles southwest of Parral, is a beautiful, fertile valley practically unknown to outsiders. The Santa Maria River rises in the Sierra and waters ranches, farms and gardens, and some of Mexico's lushest vegetables are grown here.

When the ranchers of El Valle look over their harvest of giant white potatoes, golden crisp carrots and tender green peas, they expect to meet them on their tables in proper dress. None of this thing of hurriedly boiling these beauties and dumping them in a dish. They must be properly bathed in butter and dressed in cream sauce.

2 lbs. fresh, tender green peas	3 lettuce hearts
7 tbs. butter	*Hierbas de olor*
2 firm, medium-size carrots	Salt and pepper
1 medium white potato	1 tbs. flour
2 medium golden yellow onions	½ pt. cream

Cook the green peas in just enough salted water with a pinch of bicarbonate of soda to preserve the color. Drain and set aside.

In a ceramic casserole melt four tablespoons of butter and gently introduce the carrots in long, delicate slices, the potato in small cubes, the onions chopped fine, the lettuce hearts, *hierbas de olor*, salt and pepper. Cover tightly and cook the vegetables ever so gently without water. This should take aproximately fifteen or twenty minutes.

Now add the peas and another three tablespoons of butter. Mix the flour and cream and pour in. Stir gently and allow to season and thicken over the blandest of heat for five minutes. Serves six.

Garbanzos con Pimientos
(CHICK PEAS WITH PIMIENTOS)

½ lb. garbanzos	Cooking oil
1 qt. beef stock	1 cup bread crumbs
1 can vienna sausage	Salt and pepper
3 whole pimientos	

Soak the garbanzos over night. Put on to cook in the beef stock and simmer two hours. Drop in the whole vienna sausages and cook until garbanzos are done. Add just enough moisture to keep peas from sticking. Try to end up with a pot almost dry.

When garbanzos are ready, sauté the pimientos cut in thin strips and add bread crumbs to crisp.

Drain garbanzos and sprinkle crumbs and pimientos over top. Four.

Guisado de Acelgas (SWISS CHARD CHOWDER)

Acelgas is a tricky word in Mexico. It means Swiss chard, and in most markets and on most menus the genuine article is purveyed. However the name is tacked onto spinach or the greens of mustard, turnips and beets, so, next time you are in Mexico, *caveat emptor*.

This boiled dinner is *muy Mexicana*, it is savory, and it bursts with ripe vitamins and minerals.

1 cup cooked spinach	3 tbs. cooking oil
6 medium potatoes, cooked	1 can tomato sauce
2 tbs. chopped onion	1 cup cooked garbanzos
2 cloves chopped garlic	Salt

Chop the spinach which has been cooked in almost no water, and quarter the potatoes.

Fry the onion and garlic lightly and add tomato sauce and garbanzos. Stir well, bring to a boil and serve over potatoes.

Aztec sauce goes great with the *guisado*. Serves six.

Hongos y Poblanos con Crema
(CREAMED MUSHROOMS AND GREEN PEPPERS)

Puebla, where every man, woman and child is a food *aficionado*, is the home of this dietetic triumph.

4 tbs. butter	2 dashes nutmeg
2 cups sliced mushrooms	2 cups milk
3 tbs. chopped bell peppers	1 egg yolk
1 tbs. finely chopped onion	¼ cup cream
2 tbs. cornstarch	Pimiento strips
Salt	

Melt butter in ceramic pot or frying pan and sauté mushrooms, bell peppers and onion until tender. Thoroughly mix in cornstarch, salt and nutmeg.

Pour in the milk slowly, stirring constantly, until sauce starts to simmer. Beat egg yolk and cream until homogenized and stir into sauce.

Serve sauce over toast and decorate with pimiento strips. Four.

Camote con Fruta (SWEET POTATO WITH FRUIT)

The beloved *camote* is another native of Mexico that is constantly getting itself into a stew, and it doesn't care if it is with meats, vegetables or, as in this case, with fruits.

2 sweet potatoes, cooked	2 tbs. butter
2 firm, greenish apples	3 tbs. *piloncillo* (brown sugar)
Juice 3 oranges	½ tsp. ground cinnamon
2 tsps. lime juice	

Peel and slice sweet potatoes; peel, core and slice apples. In a *cazuela* or shallow baking dish put layer of sweet potatoes, then cover with a layer of apples; repeat until all slices are used. Pour orange and lime juice over all.

Dot with butter and sprinkle on brown sugar and cinnamon.

Cook uncovered at 350° until apples are tender and top is brown, approximately half an hour.

Chayotes Exquisitos (EXQUISITE CHAYOTES)

The *chayote* is popular all over Latin America. In the United States it is little known, although it will grow as easily as a squash. One *chayote*, planted like a potato, will sprout vines which climb twenty-five feet in all direction and produce a bushel of chayotes.

A *chayote* is the size and shape of an avocado and has meat slightly firmer than a summer squash. A *chayote* can be substituted for summer squash in any dish, but because of greater character it has greater versatility than the *calabacita*.

1 onion	1 cup sweet corn kernels
2 tbs. butter	1 qt. milk
6 chayotes	Salt and pepper
5 bell peppers	Powdered Parmesan cheese

Sauté the onion slowly in butter. When it is golden add the *chayotes* peeled and quartered, the peppers cleaned and cut into thin strips and the corn.

After five minutes slow cooking the vegetables should be tender; if not, leave them on longer. Add the milk, salt and pepper; simmer slowly for half an hour. Serve immediately and sprinkle with powdered or crumbled cheese. Serves six.

Chayotes Rellenos (STUFFED CHAYOTES)

Like all subtropicals the *chayote* has such a delicate flavor that a person has to search for it. Just as it takes time and discipline to develop a taste for avocados and guavas, so it takes several helpings of *chayote* to discover the elegant but subtle savor.

6 *chayotes*	Cream or canned milk
1 medium onion, grated	1 cup bread or cracker crumbs
2 tbs. butter	(cracker crumbs are better)
Salt and pepper	

Cut the *chayotes* in half, remove the seed and cook in boiling, salted water until tender. Scrape out the meat, taking care not to break the skin.

Sauté the onion in butter. Now mix the *chayote* pulp, sautéed onion and a tiny sprinkle of black pepper. Moisten this with a little cream or canned milk to a creamy but not runny consistency.

Stuff the *chayote* shells, cover with bread crumbs and broil quickly to toast the tops, after heating thoroughly in a 300° oven.

Chiles en Nogada (STUFFED PEPPERS WITH NUTS)

This specialty of Puebla dates from 1822 when three young ladies decided to serve a dinner for their fiances with the colors of the Mexican flag—red, white and green—as their motif.

The finished dish is resplendent with green peppers rampant, parsley couchant, and red pomegranate seeds gules on a field of white cream sauce.

Such enthusiasm has grown up around this aristocrat that some Puebla housewives use 21 ingredients in the *picadillo*, or filling, and require half a day in the preparation. I have presented the short service.

12 bell or sweet peppers	Salt and pepper
½ lb. lean pork chopped fine	½ pt. cream
1 tsp. chopped onion	⅓ lb. walnut meats, blanched
2 cloves garlic chopped fine	and chopped
1 tsp. cooking oil	4 tbs. chopped parsley
½ cup seedless raisins	3 red pimientos sliced thin
5 chopped almonds	1 pomegranate
1 can tomato sauce	

Cut the stem from each pepper, clean out the seeds and disvein. Parboil the peppers until they are just tender but still firm. Take them out of the water, stuff immediately and serve hot.

The *picadillo*, or stuffing, is made by frying the meat light brown and then adding onion, garlic, raisins and almonds. Sauté a minute or two and pour in tomato sauce, salt and pepper. Simmer until it thickens and stuff peppers immediately.

Whip the salted cream, stir in chopped, blanched walnuts, parsley and sliced pimiento and ladle over each pepper. Decorate the tops with pomegranate seeds.

Col a la Norteña (NORTHERN STYLE CABBAGE)

Mexico's Northerners are miners, cowboys, goat and sheep herders and big game hunters. Whatever they do is done in a big way; consequently they eat big to maintain big energy to carry out big activity.

This light breakfast of sweet-sour cabbage and eggs, perhaps supplemented with refried beans, Mexican rolls and two or three mugs of coffee should tide one over until he gets a square meal at the *comida*.

1 firm, medium size cabbage	½ lb. chopped bacon
Salt	4 tbs. chopped onion
1 tbs. sugar	6 eggs
2 tbs. vinegar	

Slice the cabbage fairly thin and cook in boiling water with salt, sugar and vinegar. Drain and set aside.

Fry the chopped bacon and lift the meat out when it is done. In one tablespoon of the bacon fat sauté the onion; then add the cabbage and heat.

Fry the eggs, sunny side up, garnish with bacon and serve with the cabbage.

A true, hardy *Norteño* likes plenty of catsup, called *salsa Americana*, on his cabbage. Serves six.

Nabos Rellenos (STUFFED TURNIPS)

I am timid about offering this Toltec tidbit, because the turnip has apparently fallen on evil days in this country if one experience proves a straw in the wind.

I was returning from a trip with four friends when we passed a great field where thousands of large, plump turnips had just been plowed up. "Feed for the cows," my friends quickly assured me —lest I feared any such diggings would end up on my dinner plate.

I assure you, this glory of the gastronomical elite is not for the birds, nor yet for the cows; it is for the gourmet who knows his stuffings.

12 medium turnips	1 tsp. chopped parsley
1 cup chopped, cooked veal	4 tbs. butter
2 slices ham, chopped	½ cup water
1 sweet pepper, seeded and chopped	½ cup white wine, dry
1 tsp. chopped onion	Salt and pepper
1 clove garlic, chopped	1 egg yolk

Peel the turnips and cut through center just below the thick part. Hollow out the large part and stuff with a mixture of the meat, pepper, onion, garlic, parsley, salt and pepper. Put the turnips back together and secure with half toothpicks so just a tiny point sticks out. The turnips and all other vegetables are raw.

Sauté the turnips in butter; lift into a casserole and pour in water, wine, salt and pepper. Cook at least an hour in a preheated oven at 275°. Make sure turnips are tender.

Remove from oven, take a cup of liquid from casserole, beat in the egg yolk and pour over turnips. Put casserole back in oven without the top and glaze for five minutes with top broiling heat.

The turnip meat that is scooped out can be cooked in a few drops of water and butter, then mashed with cream or canned milk for the baby.

Nopalitos Rellenos (CACTUS SANDWICHES)

In April and May the cactus plants make new growth. The little leaves, or *pencos*, are light green and as crisp and tender as lettuce.

During this season, loaded burros, ox carts, wagons and trucks funnel toward the towns from barrancas and deserts with their treasure of *nopalito*. The first time I ate *nopalito*, it had been sliced and boiled with bacon, and I happily munched away believing it to be French cut green beans.

20 small, tender *nopalitos*	3 eggs
¼ tsp. soda	4 tbs. butter or oil
2 onions	1 clove garlic
¼ lb. jack cheese	1 tbs. chili powder
3 tbs. flour	½ pt. soup stock

Boil the *nopalitos* in salted water with the soda and one chopped onion. It should require five to ten minutes to cook them tender.

Remove from pot and wipe dry. Between each two *nopalitos* place a thin slice of jack cheese. Roll each sandwich in flour and dip in salted beaten eggs. Fry lightly.

Chop one onion and a clove of garlic, and chili powder and sauté gently. Add soup stock, salt and pepper and simmer until it thickens slightly.

Put the fried *nopalitos* in the sauce and heat three minutes and serve. Serves eight.

Papas Estofadas (POTATO SURPRISE)

This is a favorite hot meal in the highlands of Mexico when the potatoes are sacked and strings of garlic hang from the rafters like silver strands of pearls. As the early dusk settles and the fall rains splash on the tiles, a bowl of *estofado* serves the double purpose of fortifying the body and lightening the spirit.

1 can tomatoes, #2½	1 clove garlic, minced
1 bay leaf	Cooking oil
1 sweet pepper, chopped	1 lb. potatoes
Pinch cloves	2 slices jack cheese
Salt	Sprinkle cayenne, optional
½ onion, chopped	

Cook the tomatoes, bay leaf, pepper, clove and salt for half an hour. Run through colander.

Sauté the onion and garlic, add tomato sauce and simmer a few minutes.

Peel the potatoes, slice lengthwise and place in casserole. Pour the tomato sauce over potatoes, crisscross with sliced jack cheese, cover and cook in oven one hour at 225°. Serves four.

Pesadumbre (CHILLED VEGETABLE PLATE)

In the Mexican heraldry of herbs this brew contains the best the *curandero*, or herb doctor, has to offer. *Pesadumbre* means "sadness," although it should be "lightness," for the dish is guaranteed to chase away the blues. *Pesadumbre* has been a Lenten dish for centuries, but it also accompanies and lightens bean and meat entrees.

Observe the esoteric use of herbs: cumin strengthens the heart, laurel or bay stimulates the affections, while thyme reinforces the reins and firms the breasts. The little vegetables fortify but relax the stomach.

3 tbs. chili powder	½ lb. tender green peas
1 clove garlic	(frozen, fresh or canned)
Pinch cumin	1 lb. small new potatoes
1 tsp. thyme	1 leaf bay
1 cup vinegar	Salt
2 lbs. tiny summer squash	¼ cup olive oil

Make a sauce of chili powder, pressed garlic, cumin, thyme and vinegar; mix the sauce with the cooked, drained vegetables. Add the bay leaf and sprinkle on salt.

Let the *pesadumbre* stand covered in the cupboard for two days. Chill in the icebox two hours before serving.

Stir in the olive oil at the last moment and remove bay leaf. Garnish the serving plate with fresh jack cheese and onion rings. Serves six.

Fruta en Vinagre (PICKLED VEGETABLES)

Fruit in vinegar is really a crock of vegetables. These pickled vegetables are sold in markets and displayed in restaurants or dispensed in bars. They are excellent to eat cold and are frequently used to garnish a main dish. However *fruta en vinagre* is most

commonly cooked with a meat dish to produce something like our
pot roast.

3 medium potatoes	1 red pimiento pepper in slices
6 carrots sliced lengthwise	6 cauliflower buds
4 stalks celery	1 cucumber sliced lengthwise
4 small whole onions	Vinegar and salt
3 small, green tomatoes	1 clove garlic
1 cup cleaned string beans	1 tsp. each celery and
2 green peppers in thin slices	mustard seed

Cook potatoes until they are tender but firm; parboil carrots, celery,
onions, tomatoes and string beans for two minutes.

Soak all vegetables overnight in a brine made of ½ cup salt to one
quart water. Use only crockery, stainless steel or glass.

Drain and pack in a large container. Glass is best for viewing. Pour
in a boiling solution of ⅓ water and ⅔ white vinegar to cover. In-
filtrate with a clove garlic, celery and mustard seed and salt.

After three days the *fruta* is ready, but the contents improve with
age.

Zanahorias Rellenas (STUFFED CARROTS)

The nutritious carrot probably came to Spain from the Basque
provinces, because the word is from the difficult Basque language.

Mexicans use the carrot in many forms, but this creation is one
of the most unexpected, interesting and savory.

12 large crisp carrots	1 small onion
Cream cheese	2 cloves garlic, chopped
2 tbs. flour	2 cups carrot broth or bouillon
3 eggs	½ cup butter or oil
4 canned pimientos	Salt and pepper to taste
1 can tomato sauce	

Cook the carrots. Cut through center, scoop the heart from the
large end and fill with cheese.

Roll the small ends in flour, dip in beaten egg batter and fry lightly.

Sauté the onion and garlic very lightly and add tomato sauce; cook
five minutes. Add broth, salt and gently drop in the carrots. Add the
pimientos in long, thin strips.

Leave on heat just long enough for vegetables to pick up uniform
temperature. Serves four.

Zanahorias en Tortitas (CARROT FRITTERS)

I have heard people say they can't abide the sight of a carrot. To all such let me dedicate carrot torts. The Mexicans say, "La comida debe entrar primero por los ojos que por la boca." Food goes through the eyes before it enters the mouth.

These torts are healthful, bursting with vitamins and vigor, and tempting to the eye.

1 lb. carrots	2 eggs, separated
2 tbs. chopped onion	Salt and pepper
2 tbs. chopped parsley	2 tbs. oil
4 tbs. flour	

Peel and chop the carrots fine then cook quickly in a minimum of salted water with the onion and parsley. Reserve liquids.

Make a paste of flour and carrot water and add the beaten egg yolks. Whip the egg whites until stiff and fold into the egg paste.

Take three tablespoons of cooked carrots and two of paste and mix thoroughly to form each tort.

Fry slowly until the torts are golden brown and serve with mustard sauce. Serves four.

Tortitas de Elote (CORN FRITTERS)

In Mexico *tortitas* are generally served as a *pasta* with the *comida*, but they are excellent eaten with honey or syrup for breakfast. *Tortitas* are classically made from corn boiled on the cob and cut in thin wheels, but the sporting hazard of nibbling around the cob seems unnecessary.

1¼ cups flour	2 eggs
1 tsp. baking powder	1 cup small kernel corn,
Salt	drained
¼ tsp. paprika	

Sift flour, baking powder, salt and paprika together; add eggs and beat together well. Add corn, form into small cakes and fry in cooking oil or butter. Serves four.

Ensalada Mixta (MEXICAN MIXED SALAD)

Vegetables have been grown in Spain and Mexico for so many centuries without water that the cooks think greens should be wilted before they are fit to be served. Oaxaca, which is surrounded by a large, well-watered valley, is the only place I saw in Mexico where the market caters to what we would consider first-class vegetables.

Mexicans, generally, are not salad makers. They garnish plates with individual bits of tomato, lettuce or onion, but the elaborate mixtures of the French are unknown except in large hotels. *Ensalada Mixta* is a Mexican invention, however, that is excellent when prepared properly and chilled.

½ cup boiled potatoes in 1-inch cubes	1 tomato, sliced
	Lettuce leaves
½ cup cooked sliced carrots	½ cup cooked green beans
½ cup cauliflower buttons, cooked	chopped
	1 small cucumber, sliced
Oil and vinegar	

Put the hot potatoes, carrots and cauliflower in a shallow dish and cover with equal parts of oil, vinegar and water. Salt and let them stand for at least an hour.

Lift out the vegetables, drain and chill in the refrigerator. Slice tomato and cucumber, add other vegetables and serve on lettuce leaves. Dress with Mexican Dressing. Serves four.

MEXICAN DRESSING

Equal parts olive oil (or peanut, corn or soya) and wine vinegar. Mix with brown sugar, salt and pepper to taste.

Ensalada Angelopolitana (ANGEL TOWN SALAD)

This cooperative salad, where everyone builds his plate to suit his own taste, illustrates the Mexican saying that "food goes through the eyes before it passes the mouth." The arrangement and colors of the vegetables make the salad a thing of beauty.

1 lb. potatoes	12 each capers and black olives
4 medium carrots	1 ½ cups mayonnaise
4 medium turnips	2 tbs. prepared mustard
1 small cauliflower	Oil and vinegar
6 small sour pickles	Salt and pepper

Cook the vegetables separately until crisply tender. Quarter the potatoes, carrots and turnips and separate cauliflower into separate flowers.

Season potatoes, carrots and turnips with oil, vinegar, salt and pepper.

In the center of a platter form a small ring with the capers and seeded olives arranged around the pickles and the cauliflower ringing the capers.

Now form a larger circle with potatoes, carrots and turnips.

Mix the mayonnaise and mustard and dot it between the two outside rings. Each guest helps himself to the kind and quantity of vegetables and dressing he wishes.

Serve this salad warm—not hot—not cold. Serves six.

Coliflor con Aguacate
(AVOCADO AND CAULIFLOWER SALAD)

1 large head cauliflower
2 tbs. wine vinegar
4 avocadoes
½ cup ground almonds

10 small, crisp radishes
Salt, pepper and nutmeg
to taste

Cover cauliflower with water and cook whole in an uncovered vessel with a slice of toast on top; this reduces the strong flavor of the vegetable.

Drain and cool the cauliflower; then flavor with vinegar, salt and pepper.

Make a dressing of mashed avocadoes, ground almonds, salt, pepper and nutmeg. Cover the cauliflower with the dressing, chill and serve sliced, garnished with radishes. Salad for eight.

Ensalada de Apio (CELERY SALAD)

1 bunch celery
1 cup mayonnaise
1 chayote cooked *or* 3 firm
  white summer squash

3 tbs. chopped sour pickles
1 tbs. capers *or* green
  nasturtium seed
1 tbs. prepared mustard

Slice the celery core and the part of the root remaining in thin wheels and chop the stalks into small sections. Arrange on a platter and cover with salad dressing.

To make salad dressing mix mayonnaise with chopped summer squash and pickles, capers and mustard. Salad for eight.

Ensalada de Cebollitas (GREEN ONION SALAD)

Most truly Mexican salads are cooked, and this one is both typical and excellent.

12 tender green onions
½ lb. summer squash
3 bell peppers

3 avocados
Oil and vinegar
Salt and pepper

Chop the onions and cook them and the summer squash separately in as little water as possible. Lift the vegetables out when they are still firm but tender.

Seed the peppers and slice thin so they are almost shredded, peel and cut avocado into small chunks, slice the summer squash, add onions and mix gently. Dress with oil and vinegar about three to one, add salt and pepper, chill and serve. For eight.

Ensalada de Jitomates (TOMATO SALAD)

The person ordering from a menu in a Mexican restaurant for the first few times is in for many surprises until he learns the difference between American and Mexican food names. When a tourist asks for a tomato salad he expects sliced tomato on lettuce with a dollop of dressing, but *mire no mas,* see what he gets.

3 large avocados
Oil and vinegar
Salt and pepper

3 slices cooked ham
6 large ripe tomatoes
Lettuce

Split the avocado, remove the pit and scoop out the meat. Season the avocado with salt, pepper, oil and vinegar to taste and mash with a fork. A few drops of each is all that is necessary, but always use more oil than vinegar.

Chop the ham fine and blend well with the avocado. Slice the tomatoes fairly thin and arrange on lettuce leaves. Now spread the avocado mix over each tomato slice to cover. Salad for eight.

Ensalada de Papas y Perejil
(POTATO-PARSLEY SALAD)

This salad is simple and easy to make, yet it tastes like Mexico. It accompanies just about any meat, fish or fowl dish, or it can be served solo as a pasta course.

1 lb. potatoes	1 tbs. wine vinegar
3 tbs. chopped parsley	Salt and pepper
4 tbs. olive, soya or salad oil	

Peel and cook the potatoes. While they are still hot pour on the oil and sprinkle with salt and pepper. Mix gently; then add vinegar and mix gently again.

Warm potatoes absorb the flavors from the condiments better than do cold potatoes. The oil should be added first so it absorbs. A great salad will have a faint taste of the oil, so choose your favorite. For four.

Ensalada para Carnes Frías
(SALAD FOR COLD MEATS)

1 small head lettuce	2 medium sized, boiled
3 large, ripe tomatoes	potatoes
2 hard cooked eggs	6 radishes
	Oil & vinegar

Shred the lettuce and nest sliced tomatoes, eggs, diced potatoes and avocados sliced lengthwise. Peel the round radishes so the skin curls back to make "florecitos" or radish flowers.

Serve oil, wine vinegar, salt and pepper and let each guest anoint his own salad. The radish flower is almost a trademark of Mexican salads. Salad for six.

Hierbas de Olor (SAVORY HERB BOUQUET)

This bouquet is used when called for in a recipe, and discarded before serving.

The word "herb" is spelled indifferently "hierba" or "yerba", but the words are pronounced the same.

Tie together a bay leaf and a sprig each of thyme, marjoram and oregano and you have *hierbas de olor*.

Salsa Azteca (AZTEC SAUCE)

This is the basic sauce of Mexico even though it appears under half a dozen aliases. Its contents change as easily as the funds of an embezzled bank. This *salsa* is practically always found on the table in any home or restaurant. It is made fresh daily and is spooned into soup and over beans, meat and vegetables.

It is also called *salsa ranchera* and *salsa Mexicana*. If you wish some, just say *salsa*, and it will show up.

In this primitive mash the ingredients are mixed in a stone mortar with a pestle; this is called a *molcajete*. If you have been softened by civilization, use a food chopper.

20 chiles verdes	1 tsp. fresh coriander
20 large tomatoes	Wine glass vinegar
1 medium onion	4 tsps. olive oil
5 cloves of garlic	Salt

Stem and seed chiles and put in chopper with tomatoes, onion, garlic and coriander. Stir in vinegar and oil and salt to taste. This sauce is soupy and the piquancy depends on the blender. This is more than a day's supply if you are not a member of a large Mexican family, but will serve you and ten guests for a day to be remembered. Cut down accordingly.

Salsa de Chile y Cebollas
(ONION AND CHILI SAUCE)

This is an excellent sauce to serve over sliced roast.

2 onions	2 tbs. olive oil
1 can tomato sauce	1 tbs. wine vinegar
1 tbs. chili powder	1 tbs. chopped parsley
2 hard cooked eggs	Salt to taste

Slice the onions and cook in a covered vessel with a minimum of water. Cook the tomato sauce and chili for five minutes and add the drained onions, chopped eggs and other ingredients.

Serve immediately.

Salsa Saltillo

1 tbs. lime juice	1 clove garlic, mashed
1 onion, chopped	Salt

Either mix this sauce into a salad or rub the salad bowl with it. As you like it.

Salsa de Mostaza (MUSTARD SAUCE)

This warm hearted sauce dearly loves to spread itself for tarts, timbales or torts of fish or vegetable.

3 tbs. prepared mustard
6 tbs. olive, peanut or soy oil
  Salt and pepper

1 tbs. wine vinegar
2 tbs. chopped parsley
1 tbs. chopped onion

In a bowl whip the mustard with a fork then add the oil & vinegar a little at a time and keep mixing to get a frothy consistency. When the oil is homogenized add salt delicately; this is the real taste control.

Last of all stir in the parsley and onion. You may wish to duck the onion.

Salsa Borracha (DRUNKARD'S SAUCE)

2 tbs. chili powder
1 tbs. chopped onion
1 tbs. olive oil

2 tbs. cream bleu cheese
  Salt to taste
1 cup beer or orange juice

Mix the chili, onion, olive oil, cheese and salt until the cheese is uniform, then add beer.

Serve on most meat and fish dishes.

Salsa de Almendras (ALMOND SAUCE FOR FISH)

¼ lb. ground almonds
  Juice 3 limes
3 hard cooked eggs

1 tbs. chopped parsley
2 tbs. prepared mustard
3 tbs. salad oil

Chop the egg yolks and whites separately and mix all ingredients; salt and pepper to taste.

Seafood

Seafood

TREASURY OF THE SEA

WHAT is typical Mexican food?

The answer, of course, depends on where a person finds himself. In Puebla it is chicken *mole;* in Monterrey it is barbecued kid and fat bay beans, and in Oaxaca it is *guisado*—meat stew—and tortillas. From La Paz to the Panuco River, however, thousands of open-front cafes cater nothing but *pescado* and *mariscos.*

Mexico has more than five thousand miles of shoreline where the *pescado* and *marisco* harvest runs into hundreds of tons daily. The Mexican calls a fish a *pez* as long as it paddles through the water, but with his unanswerable logic he calls it a *pescado*—fished —the minute it has been gaffed. *Mariscos* are shell fish—abalone, clams, crab, shrimp, lobsters and oysters.

Each of Mexico's ports has its own local color and seafood specialty of which it is inordinately proud. What global gourmet could fail to thrill to the pounded abalone of Ensenada, the fileted sea bass of Guaymas or red snapper, Vera Cruz style? Who but the unadventurous would pass by the barbecue pit on the edge of San Blas without sampling the grilled mullet served on a banana leaf with coarse salt and fresh lime?

At Santiago Beach, near Manzanillo, the *aficionado* savors a fresh oyster cocktail and sips coconut juice through a straw. The sea turtle is wonderful in Salina Cruz, and the people of Tampico are so proud of their crab dishes that their baseball team is nicknamed *Los Jaibos.*

To enjoy sea food *a la Mexicana,* either in the southern Republic or at home, one needs to shuck northern caution and adopt Latin daring. Chiles are added to food for flavor, not for heat. There are more than fifty varieties of chiles used in Mexico, and only a few are hot. Introduce just a *sospecho* of chile if you wish to duck the piquancy, but be pleased to remember that chiles are about the best digestive agent known.

Clam and fish chowder, oyster stew and bouillabaisse stand high on the acceptance list in the United States, but most Americans shy away from the thought of fish soup. However a well-designed Mexican fish soup is as discreetly blended with vegetables and herbs to bring out the delicate tang of the sea as is a bouillabaisse.

So, make a pot of *caldo de pescado* and shout *"Buen provecho"* when you serve it. *"Buen provecho"* means "eat hearty."

When Spanish and English names are the same the fish is not listed here.

Atún	Tuna
Atún de aleta azul	Bluefin Tuna
Bacalao	Codfish
Bagre	Catfish
Barrilete	Skipjack
Cabrilla	Rock Bass
Cherna	Jewfish
Chile or *Quijo*	Bonefish
Dorado	Dolphin
Guachinango or *Huachinango*	Red Snapper
Jurel	Yellowtail
Lenguado	Flounder or Sole
Lisa	Mullet
Lobina Negra	Black Bass
Mero	Grouper
Mojarra	Cichlid, sunfish
Pargo	Grey Snapper
Peto	Wahoo
Picuda	Barracuda
Pez Gallo	Roosterfish
Pez Espada	Swordfish
Pez Sierra	Spanish Mackerel
Pez Vela	Sailfish (not edible)
Robalo	Snook
Sábalo	Tarpon
Sargo	Sheepshead
Tiburón	Shark
Totoaba	Mexican or white Sea Bass
Trucha	Trout
Trucha de Mar	Sea Trout

Abulón Ensenada (ABALONE ENSENADA)

The lordly abalone will live nowhere but in the brisk waters of the northern Pacific Ocean from Japan, around the Aleutians, and down western America to the middle of Baja California. He is a crusty looking univalve with a muscular foot so strong he must be pried off rocks with a bar, deep under water.

Only to the initiated will the abalone release his rare delicacy, and the chefs of Ensenada belong to the royal lodge. Ensenada faces Todos Santos Bay where the black, green and red abalone abound. To the north are extensive olive orchards and only twenty miles south lie Mexico's best wine vineyards at Santo Tomas.

Abalone is served at its best in the many seafood cafes of Ensenada, but in the Bahia it is superb.

1 lb. thinly sliced, pounded abalone	2 tbs. flour
1 cup dry white wine	2 eggs beaten
Juice one lime	Salt and pepper
	Butter for frying

Trim the "ab" around until only white meat shows, slice the meat into steaks half an inch thick. Pound each steak with the back of a hatchet or meat cleaver until the muscle is soft and broken.

Marinate in wine and lime juice ten minutes then wipe dry. Roll in egg batter and sludge lightly in flour. Fry in butter medium hot, less than a minute on a side.

Garnish plate with fresh lime and black olives. Serves two gourmets.

Adobo de Pescado (FISH WITH HERB SAUCE)

Tampico is one of America's finest seafood centers, but lacks the renown of New Orleans or Acapulco. A thousand years before oil was discovered, a fishing village sat where a city now thrives.

The giant Panuco River laps the levee in front of the Plaza, the Gulf is a dozen miles downstream, and behind the city are hundreds of ponds and lagoons. Here is the home of white cranes, blue herons, pink flamingoes and shrimp fishermen in *piraguas*.

The best time for the piscatorial pilgrim to visit Tampico is in

November, to take in the international sail fish tourney. If it is just the seafood he is after he should go in early spring, at the time of *Carnaval*—similar to the "Mardi Gras" in New Orleans.

Marimba and *mariachi* orchestras wander the streets, and the city is a symphony of music, impromptu dancing and masked revelers. *Carnaval* means *carne vale*, farewell to meat, and everyone enjoys the sumptuous seafood from Tampico. Weather is cool, and if the *norte* blows, the air is decidedly chill. That is the time to enjoy a fortifying dinner of *adobo de pescado*.

8 large slices of snapper, snook or sea bass	1 tbs. chili powder
3 tbs. cooking oil	1 tsp. ground oregano
1 ½ onions	¼ tsp. cumin
3 cloves garlic	Juice of two oranges
2 cans tomato sauce	Salt and pepper

Fry the fish lightly in oil and remove from pan. In the same oil sauté the onion which has been ground or finely chopped and minced garlic; add the tomato sauce, chili powder, oregano and cumin and simmer until the sauce thickens. Remove from heat and stir in the orange juice. Salt and pepper to taste.

In a well greased casserole put a layer of fish, cover with salsa, add another layer of fish and cover with sauce until the fish is used up. Cook for half an hour in a 350° oven.

Serve with mixed salad and hard rolls for six or eight.

Aguacates Rellenos de Camarón
(AVOCADOS STUFFED WITH SHRIMP)

Pueblo Viejo, translated "Old Town," is across the Panuco River from Tampico and may be reached by ferryboat. If you should ever cross this river of Jordan into the promised land, wear your pilgrim's weeds and approach with humility, for here is the world's shrimp Mecca.

A Mexican is always full of courtesy; he will give you his house and everything in it, and he will apologize for his humble country and imply that it is hardly fit for your scrutiny. But never, never hint to him that Marseilles or New Orleans is to be mentioned in the same breath with Pueblo Viejo.

The finest shrimp in the world, *Señor*, come from "Old Town," and the cooks know the most recondite secrets concerning their preparation.

The handsome *Tampiqueña* who guarded this secret formula had her seafood booth in the shade of a giant avocado tree beside the broad lagoon where the fishermen nightly lighted flares to lure the shrimp to their hand nets.

The secret was not hard to come by. The Señora smiled and chattered as she assembled her heavenly handiwork and told me how much of everything was necessary. The only point on which she was vague was about the mustard in the potato salad.

"Pues, Señor," she said, "One puts in the amount that is necessary."

3 large avocados	¼ cup mayonaise
1 lb. shrimp cooked and hulled	Salt and pepper
	Handful parsley
1 *chile jalapeño*, or any chile pepper in vinegar	1½ lbs. boiled potatoes
	1 cup sour cream
1 chopped, hard cooked egg	Prepared mustard to taste
2 doz. chopped green olives	Slice lime to garnish

Halve the avocados and remove the seed; carefully scrape out the pulp and save the shell. Mash the avocado and mix with shrimp, *chile jalapeño*, egg and olives all finely chopped and then blend in the mayonnaise. Add salt and pepper.

With the paste, stuff the avocado shells and decorate the top of each with a whole shrimp tail and two sprigs of parsley. Arrange on a platter with potato salad between avocados.

To make the potato salad, cut the potatoes in small cubes, salt and pepper, mix with sour cream and season with mustard.

Serve with plenty of sliced lime. Six servings.

Almejas San Quintín
(SAN QUINTIN STEAMED CLAMS)

The Japanese current, cooled in Alaskan waters, glides past the shores of western United States and bathes the beaches of Baja California with fresh, invigorating water which nurtures the finest clams in Mexico. Here are found the large gapers and pismos, so excellent in chowders, and the delicate rock and sand cockles, so subtle in flavor they should be eaten raw or cooked as simply as possible.

San Quintín Bay stretches for thirty miles along the Pacific coast, some two hundred miles south of the border. The bay is the haunt of ducks and geese, dozens of varieties of fish, lobsters, abalone, and fat, contented clams in clusters. There are no sizeable towns around the bay, but many one-woman cafes serve the harvest of the bay to the hungry traveller.

At the Cafe of the Seven Brothers I watched my feast preparing with ever sharpening appetite as a few wisps of steam escaped to smuggle out the tantalizing odors.

The cook poured a wine glass of sherry and the juice of a lime into a large kettle, added a tablespoon of butter, then cascaded in half a gallon of well scrubbed rock cockles. She put on a tight lid and set the kettle over a hot fire, and in five minutes the shell fish were popping open to release their savory juice and to steam in their own delicate vapor.

The clams were served in their shells with plenty of sliced lime, and the bowl of broth was excellent for dunking toasted Mexican rolls.

Sopa Larga, Alvarado (ALVARADO LONG SOUP)

Alvarado is a picturesque city on the mile-wide Papoloapan River some sixty miles south of Vera Cruz. The laughing, devil-may-care inhabitants have fished the surging river and the treacherous Gulf for centuries and are reputed to have the most lurid vocabularies of all Mexico. This may well be true for their godfather, Pedro de Alvarado, who boldly sailed his ship up the river and discovered their fishing village, was the most reckless of the *conquistadores*.

Today a paved highway runs from Vera Cruz to the Isthmus of Tehuantepec, and tourists cross the river at Alvarado on motor-driven ferries. While travellers wait on either bank for the ferry they are tempted into dozens of palm thatched booths that dispense shrimp and crab *charupas*, oyster cocktails, or whole fish plucked smoking from the grill and served with sliced, wild lime.

Dozens of restaurants vie with their favorite favorites, but the specialty of every chef is Alvarado Long Soup.

1 lb. snook or any large sea fish, in 1″ cubes	1 bell pepper in thin slices
	2 large ripe tomatoes, chopped
2 large onions chopped	¼ tsp. oregano
2 cloves crushed garlic	Salt to taste
4 tbs. olive oil	

Sauté onions and garlic in oil, then add pepper. When onions are light golden put all the ingredients in a clay or ceramic pot with a tight lid and boil gently for twenty-five minutes.

Serve with warm Mexican *bolillos* or french rolls. Two portions.

Arroz con Camarones (RICE WITH SHRIMP GRAVY)

Guaymas is a sun-kissed winter resort on the Gulf of California that is much visited by Mexican and American tourists who come for the unexcelled boating, fishing and sea food.

With such a select clientele to please it is no wonder that the Guaymas chefs have turned out many masterpieces. The one that seems to me to be the supreme creation is this *arroz con camarones*.

This dish may be served as a *pasta* or a main course.

4 tbs. butter	½ cup chopped mushrooms
2 tbs. flour	1 lb. small shrimp, cooked and peeled
2 cups milk	
Salt and pepper	Juice ½ lime
1 tsp. curry	3 cups *sopa de arroz* (see recipe)
2 tbs. grated onion	

Heat the butter in a ceramic vessel and dissolve the flour; add milk and stir constantly until it thickens into a white sauce. Sprinkle in salt, pepper and curry, and simmer a minute.

Add the onion and mushrooms and stir in; cook ten minutes. If the sauce is too thick add more milk. Drop in the shrimp, stir a minute and remove from fire. Add lime juice, but don't return to heat once citrus is in.

The rice, made from the *sopa de arroz* recipe, is served on a platter and the shrimp sauce poured over it. Serves four.

Arroz con Pescado (RICE WITH FISH)

1 lb. sea fish in 5 slices
4 tbs. cooking oil
2 cloves garlic
½ lb. rice
1 can tomato sauce

1 onion, chopped
1 sprig mint
Salt and pepper
1 tsp. chopped parsley

Fry the fish quickly and remove from pan; drop the garlic cloves in the hot oil and fry one minute. Discard garlic.

In the same pan, over low heat, slowly toast the rice until it turns the lightest straw color. If it is fried too hard it will not accept moisture and swell properly. Give it five to ten minutes, then add the tomato sauce, onion, mint, Tabasco, salt and pepper. Stir thoroughly.

Now bury the fish slices in the rice so there is rice below and over them. Pour in a cup and a half of hot water, jostle the rice a trifle so it is mixed. Bring to a boil, cover tightly, cut heat to lowest possible and don't lift lid for thirty minutes.

Turn out on a platter and serve hot with sprinkled parsley and lime slices. Serves four.

Bacalao a la Vizcaína (BISCAYAN STYLE CODFISH)

In the dry uplands of Spain and Mexico thousands of people have never seen a fresh fish; however they are clever at making tempting dishes from dried shrimp, sea turtle and various dried fishes.

This old codfish recipe is so good that it is usually reserved for a birthday or fiesta. Two ancient customs dictate the manner of serving *bacalao*: the cooking pot, wrapped in clean napkins, sits on the table, and the host serves directly from it; *limonada garrapiñada** is served each guest with his ration of *bacalao*.

3 lbs. dry codfish
1 cup oil
3 large slices cooked ham
3 slices bacon
3 cloves garlic

4 large onions
1 large bell pepper
1 cup breadcrumbs
3 egg yolks, hard cooked
1 dash cayenne

*For *garrapiñada* see page 172.

Cut the fish in 1 inch squares and soak over night to leach out the salt; change the water several times. After last soaking remove any scales and put on to cook without salt. Just before the water comes to a boil remove the pot from fire and pick out any bones, reserving liquid.

Making the sauce is the mark of true patience. It must not be hurried. Pour the oil in a clay pot and add the ham, bacon, garlic and onions, all finely chopped. Cook over the suavest of heat for at least two hours until the onions are puréed, then add three cups of water and cook another hour.

Put the bell pepper through a food grinder with the bread crumbs and hard cooked egg yolks; add cayenne and mix with three cups of liquid in which the codfish was heated. Pour this mixture in with the cooked onions, stir well and work through a colander.

Grease a clay *cazuela*, pour in half the sauce and bring to a boil. Slowly add the pieces of codfish, skin side up, cover with the rest of the sauce and cook slowly until the fish is tender. Move the *cazuela* now and then, or stir up the fish with a spatula so it doesn't stick to the bottom and burn.

Serve very hot and drink iced *garrapiñada* with it. Eight servings.

Camarones a La Criolla (SHRIMP CREOLE)

Criollo or *criolla* was the Colonial name for a Spaniard born in the Americas (from Mexico the word drifted to Louisiana where it took on another connotation). This *criolla* is a handsome, respectable lady who likes her shrimp in the following manner:

1 large onion, sliced fine	Salt and pepper
2 tbs. cooking oil	1 lb. cooked shrimp
1 can tomato sauce	3 tbs. capers
3 tbs. chopped parsley	12 stuffed olives, chopped

Sauté the onion without a *sospecho* of singeing, then add tomato sauce, parsley, salt and pepper. Cook five minutes.

Add the shrimp, capers and olives, along with half a cup of water, and continue cooking for twenty minutes.

Serve over white rice. Four servings.

Camarones Campeche (SHRIMP CAMPECHE)

Bring two pounds of shrimp to a boil, cut off heat and let them stand ten minutes before husking. Serve with Catalina sauce and sliced limes.

Salsa Catalina (FISH SAUCE CATALINA)

In Campeche this cooked *salsa* is used over any seafood, baked, boiled or fried, but its greatest fame comes from its use with shrimp.

2 cloves garlic, chopped	6 leaves parsley
1 onion, chopped	Salt and pepper
2 whole pimientos	⅛ tsp. each cumin & oregano
1 lb. tomatoes, raw or canned	½ cup olive oil
½ cup vinegar	

Sauté the garlic and onion in part of oil. Add the pimiento and tomatoes and immediately remove from heat. Mix in vinegar, parsley, pepper, cumin and oregano. Blend in remaining oil, salt and serve.

Ceviche San Blas

Ceviche is a mellow companion popular with the cocktail and dining crowd—both Mexican and American—from Mazatlan to Lima, Peru; however he is restricted to Pacific ports and has had to lead an amiable life to survive the canards and prejudices that have been drummed up against him.

Mexicans on the Gulf coast slyly inform listeners that when the Spaniards were conquering Mexico many fleeing natives hid out in the swamps along the Pacific. Here life was insecure and food was scarce, so the refugees were forced to eat raw fish with wild lime juice, and, in time came to imagine they liked it. Americans who have never journeyed to Acapulco or Panama and nibbled *ceviche* while sipping a tequila Marguerita, grimace in horror and exclaim, "Raw fish, bah!"

In the first place, *ceviche* is not raw; it is cooked in lime juice as thoroughly as any fish basted over fire. In the second place, if there is any credibility in the story told by the *Golfeños*, then it was an ancient Aztec prince whose noble imagination created the royal dish.

Cut up a pound of corbina or Spanish mackerel *(Pez Sierra)* in half inch cubes. In Mexico only mackerel is used, but in Central and South America corbina is considered the number one choice.

Cover the fish cubes with lime juice in an earthenware bowl and allow them to cook in the juice for four hours. No heat is applied; the citrus juice does the job chemically.

Now slice an onion and put the onion rings in the *ceviche*. Cube two tomatoes and a bell pepper with a tablespoon of vinegar and three tablespoons of olive oil, and add to *ceviche*. Toss in a pinch of oregano, sprinkle with salt and pepper and set the bowl in the ice box until the *ceviche* is thoroughly chilled.

Serve with cocktail forks at your next party and the society page will feature you as the host of the week.

Chipalchole Catemaco

Chipalchole is not a main dish; it is a light soup that is leisurely enjoyed while one chats with friends or relaxes between jobs. I savored *chipalchole* at its best in an open front cafe on the shore of Lake Catemaco. The emerald water of the lake was dotted with fishermen throwing their nets from the large dugout *piraguas*.

No one works too hard around this most beautiful of all Mexican lakes, but everyone is willing to join a friend while he loads a cart, beaches a boat or eats *chipalchole*. This is a share-the-work dish where the customer shucks the shrimp or cracks the crab claws that discreetly hide in the broth. Lime juice is squeezed into the soup and over the *mariscos*.

16 whole shrimp or 8 crab claws	1 large can tomato purée and
1 medium onion, chopped	equal amount of water
½ bell pepper in thin strips	Salt, pepper and cayenne to
Oil for sautéing	taste
2 medium potatoes, quartered	
Pinch coriander	

Lightly sauté onion and bell pepper, add other ingredients except shellfish, and boil slowly until potatoes start to soften. Drop in the shrimp or crab claws and cook another ten minutes. Serve the thin soup in low bowls with the shrimp peeking over the sides. Of course there is no law that restrains the cook from using cleaned shrimp tails or three tablespoons of crab meat if he prefers it that way. Heated hard rolls and butter complement it either way. Serves four.

Cóctel de Camarones u Ostiones, San Juan de Ulúa
(SAN JUAN DE ULUA SHRIMP OR OYSTER COCKTAIL)

Down the Pacific from Guaymas to Salina Cruz and up the Gulf from Yucatan to Matamorros, the traveller is within hail of a vendor of shrimp or oyster cocktails whenever he is in sight of blue water. Special bars dispense the fresh *mariscos* in hotels and cafes, and open front booths sit as patiently as their owners along the beaches, on the *malecones* at Vera Cruz and Tampico, and the ferry stops at Alvarado, Nautla, Tecolutla and the Panuco River.

The cocktail sauce is made from just about the same fixings all over the country. In an effort to get a good mix, I sat at my favorite *maestro's* booth by the old fort of San Juan de Ulúa in Vera Cruz. I did a surreptitious time-motion study of his sauce blending, and at the end of the two hours I had eaten four cocktails and had heisted the secret formula.

8 shrimp, cooked and shelled	½ cup catsup (Some chefs
or 8 oysters, raw	use tomato juice, others use
½ tsp. lime juice	both)
½ tsp. Lea & Perrins sauce	3 tbs. shrimp juice (for shrimp
½ tsp. finely chopped onion	cocktail only)
2 drops Tabasco Sauce	Sliced lime
2 tbs. white dry wine	

Put the shrimp or oysters in a tall glass, cover with the sauce and serve salt and pepper with heaps of sliced lime. This is one portion.

Col Relleno de Ostiones
(OYSTER STUFFED CABBAGE)

Cabbage has a natural affinity for seafood, and here it reaches its greatest hour or "col-mination."

1 large, firm cabbage	1 tsp. vinegar
1 tbs. chopped onion	Salt and pepper
2 cloves garlic	12 stuffed olives
1 tbs. chopped parsley	24 capers
2 tbs. cooking oil	18 small oysters
1 can tomato sauce	4 tbs. melted butter
1 tsp. sugar	

Cook the cabbage in salted water ten minutes and cut out the heart to accept the stuffing.

Sauté the onion, garlic and parsley; add the tomato sauce and bring to a low boil. Now stir in sugar, vinegar, salt and pepper, then the olives, capers and drained oysters cut in quarters. Allow the sauce to thicken a trifle and pour into the cabbage.

Cover the opening with two or three cabbage leaves secured with toothpicks and place in a large roasting pan. Pour the melted butter over the top, cover the pan and cook in a 300° oven for half an hour.

Serve catsup and wax peppers in vinegar on the side. Four servings.

Crema de Camarones (CREAM OF SHRIMP SOUP)

1 tsp. chives or young onions, chopped fine	4 tbs. almonds, peeled and ground
3 tbs. butter	½ lb. dry or 1 lb. fresh shrimp, ground
3 ripe tomatoes, ground and sieved	1 qt. chicken stock
1 chicken breast, ground	Salt and pepper

Sauté the chives in butter and add tomatoes; thicken for three minutes. Add chicken and ground almonds and stir in thoroughly. Drop in the shrimp and add chicken stock; season and allow to cook for twenty minutes.

Serve with toast and lime slices. Four servings.

Diablitos a Caballo (LITTLE DEVILS ON HORSEBACK)

Little Devils are frequently served as the *entremés* or first course at *comida* or *cena*. They are also wonderful appetizers at a backyard barbecue. Furnish each guest with a small skewer and let him broil his own oysters over the glowing coals while he refreshes himself with cold cider or beer.

24 large oysters
12 slices lean bacon
12 slices bread
 2 tbs. butter

Cayenne pepper
3 lemons or limes
Chopped parsley

Drain the oysters well and let them stand in lemon juice with a sprinkle of cayenne for half an hour.

Dry oysters and wrap each one in half a slice of bacon, secured with a toothpick. Skewer and broil for two minutes.

Cut the bread slices in half and fry in a lightly buttered pan; drain thoroughly on paper towels and serve oysters on the bread. Serves six.

Empanadas de Ostiones (OYSTER TARTS)

24 oysters
 2 cups flour
 1 tsp. baking powder

⅔ cup milk
2 tsps. butter
Salt and pepper

Make a biscuit dough of the flour, baking powder, salt and milk. (I use a prepared biscuit mix) Roll to a thickness of an eighth of an inch.

Cut out circles four inches in diameter. In each *empanada* place as many oysters as fit in a straight line; sprinkle oysters with salt and pepper and a pat of butter.

Double over *empanada* and pinch edges together, leaving a rippled effect.

Fry quickly on both sides in deep peanut oil and serve—listen—with heavy clotted or sour cream.

Estofado de Pescado Acapulco
(ACAPULCO FISH FEAST)

If you have ever been to Acapulco, then this *estofado* will package your memories. Here is the sunburnt mirth of Caleta and El

Horno beaches, the smooth calm of La Aguada Bay, the flaming excitement of the torch divers at night and the nostalgia of palms rustling in a tropical breeze.

1-3 lb. whole red snapper or other large sea fish	1 dozen stuffed olives
1 bay leaf	1 cup cooked peas
1 onion sliced thin	1 cup cooked and quartered carrots
2 cups tomato sauce	1 jigger brandy
Cooking oil	½ glass dry sherry
1 small can oysters	2 tbs. corn starch
1 small can shrimp	Salt and pepper

Put the fish in a large vessel with a pint of water, bay leaf, onion and salt. Boil covered about two minutes, remove from fire and let stand five minutes.

Discard the water, bay leaf and onion.

Fry the tomato three minutes, then stir in the oysters and their juice, drained shrimp, olives, peas, carrots, brandy and sherry. Make a paste of the corn starch and a little water and mix that in.

Pour the vegetables over the fish and bring to a low boil; cook until the fish is tender but is not breaking up or losing its character. Serves eight.

Filetes de Pescado con Espinacas
(FISH FILLETS WITH SPINACH)

This nutritious treat is delicate enough for the palate of a child or invalid, yet intriguing enough for the most continental of gourmets.

1 ½ lbs. sea fish fillets	Salt and pepper
Butter	2 egg yolks
2 onions	½ tsp. lime juice
½ lb. raw spinach	3 tbs. grated Gruyere cheese
1 cup milk	

Fry the fillets in butter, two minutes to a side, then add a pint of water, salt, and one onion sliced thin. Cover and bring water to boil; remove from heat, saving liquid.

In another pan sauté the other onion, chopped, in butter. Add the cleaned and chopped spinach, stir and pour in milk, salt and pepper. Cook until the spinach forms a purée.

Also make a sauce by lightly toasting the flour in melted butter and stirring in ½ pt. of the strained water in which fish cooked. Salt and pepper and cook until it thickens; remove from heat and mix in the lightly beaten eggs, lime juice and half the grated cheese.

Rub an open baking dish with butter and make a bed of the spinach purée, place the fillets on top and crown with the sauce. Sprinkle the rest of the cheese on top with specks of butter.

Lightly brown under top heat and serve immediately. Serves four.

Filetes de Pescado con Salsa de Tomate
(FISH FILLETS WITH TOMATO SAUCE)

1 ½ lbs. snook, snapper or other large sea fish	2 bay leaves
	½ pt. cream
2 limes	2 tbs. tomato catsup
Salt	1 tsp. prepared mustard
1 pt. cooking oil	3 drops Tabasco sauce
1 onion, sliced	

Stir the juice of two limes and a tablespoon of salt into a quart of water and leave the fish fillets in this water for an hour.

Remove the fish, drain and wipe. Place the fillets in a baking dish with a pint of water and a pint of cooking oil. Sprinkle the fish with salt and pepper and drop onion slices over top. Add bay leaves to liquid.

Cook uncovered in a 350° oven for half an hour. Remove fish from liquid, drain and place on platter. Cover with sauce to serve.

To make the sauce, whip the cream until it thickens and add catsup, mustard, Tabasco, salt and pepper.

Serve fish over romaine lettuce, and garnish with olives and slices of hard cooked egg. Three portions.

Garapacho de Jaiba

A few miles south of Vera Cruz, two or three miles off the highway, lies the long lagoon and fishing village of Mandingo. Dozens of dugouts and launches are tied up at the village, and four or five open front cafes specialize in the most exotic sea food in the state of Vera Cruz.

Here the shrimp and oyster cocktails are superb, the *mojarra* fish grilled over smoking coals is luscious, but the crab *garapacho* is divine.

One sunny morning before the hungry *aficionados* had started to congregate, the chef and I sat on the wide veranda overlooking the lagoon and considered two iced bottles of beer. He gave me the following recipe and while it is generous, I haven't cut it down for fear of disturbing its perfect proportion.

Meat of 8 crabs (approx. 1 lb.)	1 doz. chopped green olives
1 onion, chopped	1 tsp. capers
3 cloves garlic	2 *chiles jalapeños* or other medium hot pepper in vinegar
3 tbs. oil	2 pimientos in thin strips
1 lb. tomatoes *or* 1 can tomato sauce	Salt and pepper
⅛ tsp. each, clove and cinnamon	3 eggs, separated
1 tbs. chopped parsley	2 tbs. bread crumbs
	2 tbs. Parmesan cheese

Lightly fry the chopped onion and garlic, then add the tomato sauce and season with the spices and chopped parsley.

When the sauce bubbles, stir in the crab meat, chopped olives, capers and sliced peppers. Salt and let simmer five minutes.

Whip the whites of three eggs then beat the yolks separately. Fold the whites into the yolks.

Pour the crab mixture into a greased casserole, spoon the whipped eggs on top and sprinkle with bread crumbs. Put in a 350° oven just long enough to brown the top, powder with cheese and serve. Serves four handsomely.

Huachinango a la Veracruzana
(RED SNAPPER VERA CRUZ STYLE)

A person doesn't have to go to Newburg to get a crab Newburg, or to the Waldorf to get a Waldorf salad; neither does one have to trek to Vera Cruz for *huachinango a la Veracruzana*. In the highlands or on the beaches of Mexico the first thing a householder thinks of when he comes into possession of a big red snapper is to dress it in the flamboyant style of Vera Cruz.

A true *Veracruzano* celebrates the dinner and its attendant rites for at least two hours. He anticipates and accompanies the masterpiece with a thin red wine; afterwards he contemplates the happy occasion with more of the same *vino*. A strong minority group holds that beer is the natural accompaniment for the lordly *huachinago*.

2 lbs. red snapper or other large ocean fish in ½″ slices	12 pitted green olives
	1 wine glass dry sherry
	4 tbs. vinegar
4 tbs. lime or lemon juice	½ tsp. chili powder, ¼ tsp.
2 onions chopped	oregano, 1 piece cinnamon
2 cloves garlic sliced	bark or ⅛ tsp. ground.
2 pimientos sliced lengthwise	Pinch ground cloves
2 *chiles jalapeños* sliced, or red bell peppers or any pepper in vinegar.	2 sprigs parsley
	Salt and pepper
1 tbs. capers	2 cups tomato purée

Swab the fish with lime juice and let it stand while *recaudo* is preparing. Make the *recaudo* of sautéed onions, garlic and peppers first, then add the tomato purée and all the other ingredients except fish. Cook 15 minutes to thicken.

Lay the fish in a casserole and pour the sauce over it. Cover the casserole and cook briskly for twenty minutes at 350°. Check constantly to see that nothing sticks or burns.

Start off with a cup of consommé, then serve the fish with a large bowl of Mexican fried rice. Load the board with toasted Mexican or French rolls, butter and a heap of sliced lime or lemon. In Mexico lime juice is squeezed into consommé as well as over fish.

After the meal is finished give each diner a small cup of coffee— very hot and very strong—and he will need only *marimba* players tinkling a tune to make him think he's on the Malecon. Nourishes four.

Jaibas Rellenas (STUFFED CRAB)

I had this recipe from the cook in one of the fine seafood cafes that dot the wide sand beaches in Tecolutla, Vera Cruz. He used a dozen of the medium sized *jaibas* that scuttle about the mouth of the mile-wide Tecolutla River.

It is patent one will have to use his judgment in this matter, for a dozen Dungeness or King crabs would take care care of the noon rush at many a cafe. Therefore, if only fairly large crabs are available select one for each guest and start creating. This is for eight people.

2 cups crab meat. Reserve shells.
2 tbs. chopped onion
Cooking oil
1 can tomato sauce
1 pimiento, chopped
10 pitted green olives
3 tbs. ground almonds
1 tsp. prepared mustard
2 drops Tabasco sauce, or to taste
Salt and pepper
½ cup breadcrumbs
2 hard cooked eggs, chopped
2 tbs. butter

Remove claws and cut out top of shell. Clean well. There is a little meat in the shell, but most is in the claws. Crack and recover meat and shred or chop it fine.

Sauté the onion, add tomato sauce, chopped pimiento and olives, ground almonds, mustard, Tabasco, salt and pepper and half the bread crumbs. Cook until it thickens almost to forking consistency and remove from fire. Stir in the two eggs well chopped and stuff the crab shells or place in baking shells.

Sprinkle bread crumbs over tops and dot with butter. Place in broiler and brown quickly and serve.

This provender calls for sliced limes and plenty of cold beer.

Mexico's Lake Fish

Lake Patzcuaro is on of the most charming and picturesque regions of Mexico. Here the fishermen in their dugouts seine the remarkable whitefish with their graceful butterfly-shaped nets. In the middle of the lake is the island of Janitzio. It was on this island that I sat high up on one of the steep streets and watched the life on the lake while I savored Mexico's great delicacy—whitefish. The ancient, cobbled towns of Patzcuaro and Quiroga sit on the shores of the lake where they can be reached by paved road. These towns also feature the famous whitefish and mellow charm.

The only other place where the *pescado blanco* thrives is in Lake Chapala, a hundred and fifty miles to the west. Chapala is sixty miles long and half covered with water hyacinth, but it fails to match Patzcuaro for its beauty or quality of fish.

In the town of Chapala, thirty miles from Guadalajara, boys sell dried *charales*, an almost transparent fish that is considered locally as a natural hors d'oeuvre with tequila. Chapalans are also fond of the carp and catfish that abound in the lake; but actually the only authentic specialty of Chapala is *El Caldo Michi*, a delicious catfish soup, made as follows:

2 lbs. catfish cut in large chunks	Pinch coriander
3 chopped onions	Sprinkle of cayenne
½ bell pepper thinly sliced	Salt and pepper
6 skinned and chopped tomatoes	

Sauté onions and pepper, then add tomatoes, coriander and cayenne. Pour this *recaudo* into a quart of boiling water, drop in fish, salt and pepper. Cook for thirty minutes and you'll have a *caldo* as placid as the lake on a sunny day. Serves six.

Ostiones Alvarado (ALVARADO STYLE OYSTERS)

One must be virile and vigorous to survive in Alvarado, but this oyster stew would be number one in any survival kit.

1 medium onion	¼ tsp. oregano
1 clove garlic	Pinch cayenne
3 tbs. chopped bell pepper	2 medium potatoes
Sprig parsley	2 doz. fresh oysters
3 tbs. cooking oil	1 tsp. vinegar
2 cups tomato purée	Salt and pepper
Pinch clove	½ cup bread crumbs
⅛ tsp. cinnamon	

Sauté the onion, garlic, chopped pepper and parsley, then add the tomato purée and bring to a boil. Mix the spices with the oyster juice and stir into the *recaudo;* cut the potatoes in medium chunks and introduce them to the warm hearted group.

Cook until the potatoes are done and interpolate the oysters and vinegar. Remove the pot the instant it comes to a boil. Pour the stew into a casserole, top with crumbs and a few drops of oil and leave in a 350° oven until the crumbs brown. Feed immediately to four famished fishermen.

Paella Valenciana

Paella is a proud old Mediterranean dish that was undoubtedly brought to Spain by the Moors, yet it is as much at home in Mexico as a tamale. It is discreetly flavored, full bodied and so highly socialized that it will immediately make friends with any other food at the same table.

An abandoned silver mine in Guanajuato and its gold-plated baroque church stand as silent memorials to the continuing greatness of *paella.* In 1554 some workmen cleared a small work area on a hillside and started a fire to cook a pot of *paella;* the fire melted tiny particles of silver and one of Mexico's richest mines was discovered and named appropriately enough, La Valenciana.

Another place that features the aristocratic old name is Cafe La Paella on Constitution Plaza in Vera Cruz. Here *paella* is served daily as a *pasta.* The lofty and uncomplaining manner in which it plays a supporting role to dishes without a tenth of its breeding proves the noble humility of *paella.*

1 small onion chopped	2 tbs. crab meat
1 pimiento in thin slices	1 doz. small clams, fresh or
Oil	canned
1 qt. chicken soup	1 cup peas
2 cups uncooked rice	2 sprigs parsley, chopped
1 cup chicken in ½″ cubes	Pinch saffron
1 lb. shrimp, raw or canned	Salt and pepper

Sauté the onion and pimiento until the onion is light gold; add to the chicken soup and bring to a boil. Stir in the rice and add all other ingredients and cook thirty minutes over low heat. Serve four on plates; *paella* should not be soupy.

If you wish to capture the true, unspoiled smack of a dish which was originally eaten with the fingers, then you will use well scrubbed clams in their shells, crab claws and shrimp tails with the hulls still on. Each diner cracks his own seafood.

Pescado a la Jarocha (SEA FISH TAMPICO)

A woman from Tampico is a *Jarocha*, and she knows her *mariscos* and *pescados* as well as any cook in the world. When it comes to seafish supreme she will stake her reputation as a cook on this simple method.

2 lbs. sea fish fillets	3 tbs. thick, fresh cream
Juice one lime	1 cup mayonnaise
Oil	24 black olives, sliced
Salt and pepper	1 tsp. chopped parsley

Rub the fillets well with the juice of one lime and oil; then sprinkle with salt and pepper. Bake uncovered for fifteen minutes in a preheated 450° oven and turn out onto a platter.

Mix the cream, mayonnaise, olives and parsley and spread on each fillet. Serves four.

Pampano Pohchuc (GRILLED POMPANO)

This simple recipe with its Mayan name is followed through Yucatan, Campeche and the Isthmus of Tehuantepec. Pompano is a highly prized fish. It is featured in the best eating houses as far north as New Orleans and San Francisco.

The marinade here is for one ten-inch fish; stretch it out to cover your needs.

1 pompano or other small delicate fish	1 tbs. salt
½ tsp. freshly ground black pepper	½ cup sour orange juice *or* ⅓ lime juice and rest orange juice
1 clove garlic, pressed	

Clean and scale pompano. Mix other ingredients and marinate fish for an hour; wipe off thoroughly and grill over coals. Be sure to wipe grill with peanut oil, so fish will not stick. High heat will tear fish. Heat should be low, slow and consistent.

Serve a large bowl of guacamole and quartered, toasted tortillas.

Pescado con Chile y Vino Tinto
(CHILI FISH IN RED WINE)

This is one of the many Mexican dishes that must stand from one hour to three days to bring out the subtle nuances of the herbs and seasonings. Observe that none of the ingredients are hot, strong or overbearing; all are as sweet, small and delicate as singers in a children's chorus.

2 lbs. sliced ocean fish	½ cup olive oil
1 tbs. chili powder	1 cup red, dry wine
2 cloves garlic	2 tbs. chopped parsley
1 tsp. cumin	24 green olives
1 can tomato sauce	24 capers
1 sweet pepper in thin strips	Salt, pepper and oregano

Mix all ingredients except the fish to form a savory *recaudo*, but go easy on the oregano until you learn your own tolerance.

Arrange the fish slices in a narrow, deep casserole, pour the *recaudo* on top, cover and cook at 350° until done.

Let casserole cool down, then reheat and serve. Serves four.

Pescado con Naranja (ORANGE BAKED FISH)

8 slices fish	Cooking oil
Salt and pepper	2 tbs. chopped parsley
Lime juice	1 cup bread crumbs
4 cloves garlic	½ cup orange juice

Rub the fish with salt, pepper and lime juice. Press the garlic and mix with oil, parsley and salt. Bathe the fish slices in the oil then roll in bread crumbs. Brown quickly.

Stash the fish slices in a high, narrow casserole, pour in orange juice and bake at 350°, covered, for 50 minutes. Eight, if slices are large.

Pescado con Salsa de Higaditos
(FISH WITH CHICKEN LIVER SAUCE)

Creative imagination and an unexpected compatibility of taste bud ticklers were parents to this handsome *entrada*.

8 fillets of fish	3 tbs. peanut oil
1 bay leaf	1 tsp chopped onion
1 green onion, chopped	1 clove garlic, optional
1 slice lime or lemon	1 sweet pepper or pimiento
2 tbs. olive oil	1 cup tomato purée
6 chicken livers, cooked	Pinch each clove, cinnamon,
1 bread slice	pepper
¼ cup water and vinegar, equal	Salt
parts	

Cook the fish slowly and covered in a tiny bit of water with the bay leaf, chopped green onion, slice of lime and olive oil.

To make the sauce grind the cooked livers with the bread soaked in vinegar water. Heat the peanut oil and sauté onion, garlic and finely chopped sweet pepper; add tomato purée and liver-bread paste. Season and cook five minutes.

Lift and drain fish carefully so as not to break fillets, place on a platter and spread sauce evenly over slices and serve. Serves eight.

Pescado de Navidad (CHRISTMAS FISH)

Pescado de Navidad is the Christmas goose of Mexico, especially in the coastal regions. This platter requires time and loving care, but it is worth any effort. The end result is the triumph of Tampico's time-tested recipes.

1 seafish—2 to 3 lbs.	2 small cans shrimp
5 limes	1 can asparagus tips
Salt and pepper	4 hard cooked eggs
1 can red pimientos	Cooking oil
2 onions	2 bay leaves
Small bottle stuffed olives	Mayonnaise
3 tbs. chopped parsley	

The fish should be cleaned and scaled with head and tail removed; with a sharp knife and pliers split the back and remove backbone and any large stray bones.

Soak the fish for an hour in a quart of water in which a tablespoon of salt and juice of two limes has been mixed.

Dry thoroughly and rub inside and out with salt and pepper and the juice of a lime. To stuff the fish make the following dressing.

Finely chop one can shrimp, six asparagus tips, one hard cooked egg, two pimientos, one onion, a third of the stuffed olives and three sprigs of parsley. Mix thoroughly. Sounds good, doesn't it?

Stuff the fish and sew it together with needle and white thread.

Butter the inside of a baking dish and place the fish in it. Put half a cup of water and half a cup olive oil, or other cooking oil, salt and pepper, bay leaves, one onion sliced, and the juice of two limes. Cover and cook at 350° until done, about forty-five minutes.

Remove to a platter, pull off the skin and allow the fish to cool. Cover well with mayonnaise and adorn with strips of pimiento, grated hard-cooked egg yolks and whites, olives and shrimp. The pimiento strips are arranged to form poinsettias with the green olives in the center.

This calls for lots of chilled white wine, and is considered a cool cold buffet. Serves six to eight.

Pescado en Escabeche (MEXCAN PICKLED FISH)

Fry eight fairly thick slices of ocean fish such as red snapper, tuna, snook or swordfish until it is brown on both sides but not cooked through. Place the fish in *escabeche*, and as the sauce starts to boil remove from fire and cool. Carefully lay the fish slices in a crock, taking care not to break them, and pour in the *escabeche*.

A Mexican cook always says the fish should stand at least two days before serving; however the *pescado en escabeche* will keep for several weeks.

Serve the *pescado* cold with a garnish of olives and lettuce.

Escabeche

Escabeche is a vinegar sauce that is used to pickle meat, fowl and fish, or it may be served cold as a side dish at the table. Over baked, roast or fried meat or fowl no oil is used in the *escabeche*, but with freshly baked or fried fish, olive oil is added.

6 *chiles cuaresmenos* (wax peppers in vinegar) sliced lengthwise and seeded
2 large bell peppers in slices
2 large white onions, sliced
2 cloves garlic, crushed
2 bay leaves

1 pt. vinegar
1 heaping tablespoon salt
⅛ tsp. cumin
½ tsp. oregano
¼ tsp. black pepper
1 cup olive oil (to add to fish only) 2 tbs. oil for frying others.

Fry the peppers, onion and garlic in olive oil at low heat until onion is soft; add all other ingredients and bring to a boil. As *escabeche* starts to boil set aside and let cool; it is better after it has stood at least 24 hours.

Pescado en Salsa de Avellanas
(FISH IN FILBERT SAUCE)

This Gulf Coast favorite ranges from Tampico to the border, but it is at its nutty best in Matamorros, across the Rio Grande from Brownsville, Texas. It is well known in many of the smarter seafood centers of Texas where the filbert is nobility.

8 fish fillets or steaks
2 cups white, dry wine
1 green onion
1 bay leaf
Sprig each oregano, thyme, marjoram
3 tbs. olive oil or soya oil

1 slice bread
20 filberts
1 tbs. chopped parsley
1 clove garlic
Pinch saffron, if you can get it
Salt and pepper

Cook the fish in a covered pot with wine, chopped green onion, bay leaf, oregano, thyme and marjoram.

Heat the oil and fry the bread. Remove and grind with the filberts roasted and peeled, parsley, garlic and saffron. Stir the filbert paste into the hot cooking oil and add the strained wine in which the fish was cooked.

Cook the sauce for five minutes and pour over the fish.

The saffron yellow of this sauce holds the spotlight at any table, and the flavor retains the memory. Serves six or eight.

Pescado en Salsa de Chiles Poblanos
(FISH IN SWEET PEPPER SAUCE)

In Spanish one can differentiate between foods hot from the fire and foods hot from spices, whereas in English both are called "hot." B.T.U. hot is *"caliente"* while pepper hot is *"picante."*

Fish is quite generally served cold with sauce, but here is a savory variation in which you have hot fish and hot sauce; that is, *pescado caliente con salsa caliente.* Actually both sauce and *pescado* are as sweet and gentle as a maiden's kiss.

2 lbs. fish, whole or sliced	1 tbs. chopped onion
10 large sweet peppers	5 uncooked egg yolks
½ cup olive or peanut oil	2 cups water
2 cloves garlic	Salt

Clean, seed and grind the bell peppers. Heat the oil and fry the garlic whole; remove garlic from oil and discard it; fry the onion and ground peppers in the oil.

When the peppers are well done, remove from pan, cool and mix in the egg yolks, water and salt. Heat in a double boiler and hold just at boiling for ten minutes.

Fry or bake the fish to your taste and pour the sauce over it and serve.

Sliced lime, refried beans and cold beer go with this fish fry. Four.

Pescado Pohchuc

The famous fishing town of Campeche lies on the west coast of Yucatan where it was once part of the Mayan Empire. Mayan customs and Mayan words float through the town's daily life like driftwood around an eddy. *Pohchuc* is a Mayan word, and *Pescado Pohchuc* means broiled fish. The preparation, however, is as uncomplicated as the soft-voiced Mayan fishermen.

1 large baking fish	Salt and pepper
3 tbs. lime juice	Oil
1 clove garlic crushed	

Split the fish lengthwise and remove the backbone. Make four cuts crosswise on both slices and marinate about an hour in the lime juice, garlic, salt and pepper. (Marinate by rubbing fish thoroughly on all sides and letting stand.) Rub the fish with oil on both sides and broil quickly.

Put the slices together and slice crossways to serve. Pour *escabeche* over the *pohchuc*, furnish lots of crumbly white cheese and you have a Mayan feast. Serves four.

Pescado Sorpresa (FISH SURPRISE)

This is a great surprise party for leftover fish.

4 slices smoked bacon	Salt and pepper
1 lb. cooked, flaked fish	Bread crumbs
1 cup white sauce	2 hard cooked eggs
3 cups mashed potatoes	1 tbs. chopped parsley

Fry the bacon and cut in small pieces. Mix bacon, fish and white sauce evenly.

In a shallow baking dish spread the potatoes and leave a valley in the middle. Fill the valley with fish sauce mix, and sprinkle bread crumbs on top; dot with small pats of butter.

Brown quickly under top heat and dress with egg slices and parsley. Serves four.

Pulpos Borrachos (DRUNKEN SQUID)

In your travels you may one day find a squid in your possession. Petty prejudice will press you to get rid of it, but don't be prompted by propaganda.

Squid is a delicacy *numero uno* to millions of Chinese, Pacific Islanders and Latin Americans, and a hundred million of such fine people can't be wrong.

Try this recipe and you'll agree with the Chinese, who say: "I love my wife, but oh, you squid!"

2 lbs. squid meat	Cooking oil
½ cup brandy	1 cup dry red wine
1 large onion	4 cans tomato sauce
2 cloves garlic	Salt and pepper
2 tbs. chopped parsley	

Pound the squid thoroughly with a wooden rolling pin and put on to soak for an hour in brandy and salt. Add barely enough water to cover and boil until tender. Lift out the squid and cut into small pieces and save the broth.

Sauté the onion, garlic and parsley; then add the tomato sauce and cook five minutes. Now add the squid to the tomato sauce along with the broth, wine, salt and pepper and simmer half an hour.

Serve with olives, capers and red wine. Enough for six.

Robalo en Escabeche Colorado
(PICKLED SNOOK IN RED SAUCE)

Robalo en escabeche is a good novelty dish to serve for a luncheon on a hot day or any time the occasion has a Mexican motif. Serve the fish on a large white platter and garnish with parsley, and there are the Republic's colors: red, white and green.

3 lbs. snook or other large ocean fish	4 tbs. chili powder
	4 cloves garlic
1 glass vinegar	

Slice the fish crosswise in pieces and fry on both sides until done; then pack the fish as closely as possible in a bowl.

Press the garlic and mix well with vinegar and chili powder; add enough hot water so the *escabeche* just covers the fish. Allow to stand twenty-four hours and serve cold.

The fish gets lonely unless a smoking platter of *frijoles refritos* accompanies it. Serves six.

Tallarines con Camarones al Chino
(CHINESE STYLE SHRIMP AND NOODLES)

Chinese servants and slaves were brought to Mexico during all of the seventeenth century on the Manila Galleons. Since then a steady trickle has been arriving. Today the Chinese are found all over Mexico, but their greatest influence is on the West Coast.

They go about their business of running laundries and restaurants with Oriental imperturbability and speak Spanish with a Chinese accent. They call *camarones*, "camalones," but they are masters of dressing "shlimp," whatever they call them.

1 lb. fresh, peeled shrimp, quartered	1½ tbs. sherry
¼ onion	1 tbs. soya sauce
½ lb. dry noodles	1 cup spinach, cooked and chopped
3 tbs. olive or peanut oil	1 tbs. chopped parsley
1 tbs. corn starch	Salt and pepper

Sprinkle the raw shrimp with salt and pepper and let them stand while the noodles are cooking. Put a quarter onion in water and bring to boil, then salt; drop in the noodles and cook until tender. Drain.

Heat two tablespoons of oil in a ceramic casserole and stir in the corn starch; mix in the wine and soya sauce and add spinach and shrimp. Mix. Cook fairly hot for three minutes until the shrimp turn a deep rose.

Pour the drained noodles in with the shrimp, mix together well, add the last spoon of oil, cover and cook another ten minutes. Season and sprinkle with parsley. Serves six.

Tortilla con Camarones (SHRIMP TORTILLA)

½ lb. fresh or canned shrimp	2 tbs. cooking oil
6 eggs	½ lb. almonds, blanched and ground
¼ cup milk	
Salt and pepper	

Cook and shell the shrimp and finely chop half of them.

Beat the eggs well, stir in the milk and add salt and pepper. Heat and oil a large frying pan and start the eggs cooking over slow heat.

When the bottom half of the eggs is cooked thick, sprinkle the chopped shrimp on top and half the ground almonds. Fold like an omelet and lift out on a platter. Sprinkle the remaining almonds over the *tortilla* and garnish the plate with shrimp and serve. Four servings.

NOTE: The bottom half of this dish should be quite firm, and the top half solidified, but extremely tender when it is folded over.

Antojitos Mexicanos

Antojitos Mexicanos

MEXICAN WHIMSIES

ANTOJITOS are simple, one-dish treats that a Mexican usually eats between meals, at bus stops and fiestas or while watching a bull fight. They are the dishes that Americans think Mexicans live on, just as foreigners believe that we eat nothing but hot dogs, apple pie with cheese or ham and eggs. Tamales, tacos and enchiladas are the best known *antojitos* in the United States.

The word *antojito* means *"little antojo."* An *antojo* is a spur-of-the-moment desire. When a pregnant woman wants a slice of watermelon at three o'clock in the morning of January fifteenth that is *antojo*.

Some *antojitos* are seasonal. They may only appear at certain times of the year or when special crops ripen, but generally they are in supply the year around. Nearly every cafe in the Republic specializes in one or more *antojitos* while certain shops vend nothing else; however, most sales are made by women and girls who set up charcoal braziers on street corners or maintain booths in markets and at fairs.

There is little uniformity in shapes and ingredients used in the little whimsies. If I tell you that a *charupa* is oval shaped and open faced and a Mexican tells you it is round and folded, please remember the most typical saying in Mexico: *No hay reglas fijas*—there are no fixed rules. The one thing you can be assured of is that most *antojitos* are made with corn, called maiz, which is prepared the same way from Lower California to Yucatan.

The corn is soaked in hot, but not boiling, lime water for twenty-four hours then ground on the stone *metate* to form *masa*. The *masa* is damp enough to hold together when it is patted into pancake shaped tortillas, but absolutely nothing is added to the ground corn. A good *tortillera* slaps rather than pats the corn cakes, and she stays with the *masa* until it has character. My son, Jimmy, and I did a time-motion study in a market and the *masa* molder averaged forty-five pats per tortilla.

The tortillas are quickly and lightly baked on a metal or clay *comal* without shortening.

Incidentally, international dietetic agencies have found that *masa* is the best known source of lime to form strong teeth. The only Mexican I ever saw with bad teeth had been cooking for Americans for forty years.

To make certain *antojitos* the *masa* is patted into different shapes and sizes and quickly fried in deep fat then drained. Paradoxically enough, deep frying seals the surface and leaves less residual grease than sautéing in a thin skim of oil.

American corn meal cannnot be used in creating *antojitos*, but most large markets sell *masa*. The best way to enjoy the little goodies is in Mexico where you watch them made.

BREAKFAST BEVERAGES

Café con leche is the standard way of serving coffee in Mexico. Make a pint of coffee quadruple strength, heat milk almost to boiling and pour a third of a cup of coffee and fill with hot milk. At first you may not like this, but it grows on one with time as does any art.

For Mexican chocolate make a pint of hot chocolate, add a quarter teaspoon of cinnamon and whip until it is frothy.

Atole is made by mixing *masa* into milk, straining then boiling for half an hour and adding sugar and a pinch of cinnamon. If a square of bitter chocolate is mixed with *atole*, it becomes *champurrado*. A woman who owned a restaurant in Cuernavaca showed me how to make *champurrado* in a manner practical for any gringo. For each cup of milk, mix in a teaspoon of chopped bitter chocolate, one and a half teaspoons of corn starch, sugar and cinnamon to taste. Cook the *champurrado* in a double boiler for half an hour.

Budín de Tortilla y Picadillo
(TORTILLA AND MEAT SAUCE PUDDING)

This tasty *budín* can be eaten as an *antojito* or served as a *pasta* with the *comida*.

12 tortillas	*2 cups *mole* sauce
*3 cups *picadillo*	Cooking oil

Drop the tortillas in deep, hot oil and fry five seconds on a side, so they do not crisp or toughen.

Cover the bottom of a greased baking dish with a layer of tortillas then spoon *picadillo* on top and *mole* over the sauce. Make another layer of tortillas and continue until ingredients are expended.

Put strips of cream cheese on top and heat in oven until cheese is thoroughly melted.

Either cut through *budín* with a sharp knife and serve like a layer cake or serve individual tortillas with the goodness on top. Serves six.

Charupas del Paseo de San Francisco
(CHARUPAS OF SAN FRANCISCO DRIVE)

Charupas are open-faced and built on oval shaped tortillas about five inches long and served with red or green sauce. They seem to like the highlands of central and eastern Mexico with the shrine of their greatest devotion in Puebla. The *charupa*, like all *antojitos*, may be stacked with about anything handy that will sit on the same tortilla with tomato *salsa*. I have eaten them with onion and hot mashed potatoes.

In Puebla, where cooking is a fine art, every chef is a high priest and each diner is an expert. My favorite street is 3 Poniente—West Third—a modern street blocks away from the bustling centers of commercialized tourist traffic. In a leisurely stroll down this avenue one passes every type of store he can wish for, a winery, the Convent of St. Augustine, and a fountain-cooled park. In any one of a dozen super clean cafes he can fortify himself with the famous *charupa* which years ago left ancient San Francisco Drive to help make the entire city famous.

Making the *charupa* is simplicity itself. Pat out the oval tortillas

*See the recipes in this book for *picadillo* and *mole*.

or snip them from commercial tortillas with a pair of scissors. Prick tiny holes in one side for butter to enter and fry the *charupa* on both sides in a dry pan. Chop together half a pound of pork roast with a clove of garlic and half an onion and fry without oil.

Lay the *charupas* in a hot bake pan and pour half a spoon of melted butter over each followed by red or green *salsa*. Sprinkle with the hot pork and cover with chopped green onions

Chilaquiles Poblanos

For several weeks I stayed in a resort hotel in Western Mexico. A moving picture company was on location nearby, and their lovely feminine star stayed in the same hotel.

I observed that the gorgeous creature dearly loved *chilaquiles* and eggs, in fact she ordered them every morning for breakfast. I also observed, some weeks later when she had returned to the capital, a small item in a movie column that the star was fighting her waist line.

10 tortillas	1 clove garlic, pressed
1 can tomato sauce	Pinch clove
1 seeded pickled pepper, ground	½ lb. chorizo or sausage
	Salt and pepper
¼ onion, chopped	

Heat the tomato sauce and add pepper, onion, garlic juice, clove, salt and pepper. Cook five minutes.

Cut or tear the tortillas into random bits no more than one inch on a side and fry in oil until they are soft but not crisp.

In another pan crumble and fry sausage until done.

Now put the hot *chilaquiles* on the bottom of a platter and pour the tomato sauce on top. Add the fried chorizo or sausage and mix into the sauce; sprinkle with ground Parmesan cheese.

Serve with slices of onion and avocado on top and, if you wish, fried eggs on the side. Six servings.

Chiles Rellenos Juan Rodriguez
(STUFFED PEPPERS JUAN RODRIGUEZ STYLE)

Juan Rodriguez owns the modern but authentically Mexican Manhattan Cafe across the street from Hotel Fenix in Guadalajara. Juan serves each guest a free Manhattan cocktail on Sundays and holidays and purveys the world's best *chuletas de cerdo en parilla*—grilled pork chops—every day.

When I asked Juan for the secret to his delicate *rellenos* he instructed one of his cooks to give me the recipe. She told me, "You put the little words down, Señor; I don't write." Here are the little words.

6 long green peppers, called Anaheim chiles in California	*Sauce*
	2 tbs. chopped onion
	1 tbs. peanut oil
1 small cream cheese	1 ½ cups tomato sauce
3 eggs, separated	¼ tsp. oregano
½ cup flour	Salt and pepper
Oil for frying	

Slit peppers at lower end and remove seeds and pulp but leave on stems. Parboil until tender and stuff each pepper with two pieces of cheese ⅛ inch thick.

Separate the eggs and beat the whites until they are like snow then add yolks and continue beating until uniform and fluffy; salt egg batter.

Heat oil in pan, roll chilis in flour then dip in egg batter and fry until egg is golden. Pour sauce over each *relleno* and serve.

To make the sauce, sauté the onions in oil, add tomato sauce, salt and oregano and simmer five minutes. Serves four.

Chiles Rellenos, Puebla style

Puebla style *chiles rellenos* are similar to the stuffed peppers we make in the United States. The *chile poblano* is close enough to our sweet or bell pepper that one can be substituted for the other.

12 large bell peppers	*Sauce*
1 qt. *picadillo* (see recipe)	2 onions, chopped
1 cup flour	3 tbs. peanut oil
3 eggs, separated	3 pts. tomato sauce or drained tomatoes
Oil for frying	
	1 cup shredded yellow cheese
	Salt and pepper

Slit the peppers down the side, clean out and wash. We usually cut a round hole in the top for the operation. Fill the peppers with *picadillo,* roll in flour, dip in egg batter as in preceding recipe and fry.

Put the *rellenos* in an open pyrex dish, pour in tomato sauce, made as in the previous recipe, cover peppers with shredded cheese and cook uncovered in a medium oven until peppers are tender.

Chorizo Mexicano (MEXICAN SAUSAGE)

Chorizo gives that *yo no sé qué* to food that we call a true Mexican flavor. It is not to be eaten alone nor yet used in other dishes with a heavy hand, but dispensed judiciously. It is a true chef's helper.

This sausage is easy to make, so, if the markets in your part of the country don't stock chorizo, stuff a few links of your own. It will keep for weeks in a cool, airy place.

2 lbs. ground lean pork
½ lb. vegetable shortening
3 tbs. chili powder
2 bell peppers, ground
2 tbs. paprika
1 pint wine vinegar
½ cup 100 proof brandy
1 tsp. coarsely ground pepper

½ tsp. each cinnamon and cloves
¼ tsp. each ginger, nutmeg and coriander seed
1 tsp. each oregano, cumin and thyme
8 cloves garlic, pressed
6 bay leaves, crumbled
Cellophane casing

Mix the shortening into the meat very thoroughly then add all the other ingredients and work for at least five minutes.

Now put it in a crock or porcelain bowl, covered, and let stand twenty-four hours.

Stuff into casing one inch in diameter and pack tightly; tie off every four inches.

Hang up in a cool, airy place and chorizos will be ready to use in twenty-four hours.

Enchiladas Ameca-Meca Style

Ameca-Meca sits on a high saddle between the 17,000 foot snow-covered peaks of Popocateptl and Ixtaccihuatl. The town, which enjoys a bracing climate and the coldest city water in Mexico, is the jumping off place for climbers scaling the famous peaks.

12 tortillas	1 level tsp. chili powder
½ lb. lean pork, roasted	Pinch each of coriander,
2 *chorizos* (Mexican sausages)	nutmeg, clove, cinnamon,
2 onions, 1 chopped, 1 ground	thyme, pepper, and salt.
2 tbs. chopped parsley	1 cup peanut oil
2 *chiles jalapeños* or green	12 stuffed green olives
peppers in vinegar	1 tbs. capers (or green nast-
¼ lb. yellow cheese, grated	urtium seed soaked in
	vinegar)

To make the filling, fry together the shredded roast pork, ground sausage, the chopped onion, parsley, and seeded chiles. Remove from pan and mix *half* the grated cheese.

Make a *salsa* by mixing the ground onion with chili powder and spices.

Fry each tortilla lightly in oil before filling with meat mixture. Top with a little sauce, roll, and fry for about thirty seconds in hot oil. (Use tongs to prevent burned fingers) Drain on paper napkins, sprinkle with remaining cheese and garnish with olives and capers.

Enchiladas

Enchiladas are easy to make, but their excellence depends largely on the filling and sauce used. A good deal of originality can be achieved by varying colors and flavors in the fillings and toppings. Here are some excellent combinations

CREAM ENCHILADAS

12 tortillas	2 *chilpotle chiles* or wax
2 cooked chicken breasts	peppers in vinegar (if not
⅓ lb. cream cheese	available use 1 tsp. vinegar
Salt and pepper	and ½ tbs. chili powder)
1 cup cream	¼ lb. butter
Gruyere cheese	

Chicken breast, called *pechuga*, is the aristocrat of Mexican food, so treat it reverently. Section the chicken meat and mix lightly with finely sliced cream cheese. Stir salt, pepper, and finely chopped, seeded peppers into the cream.

Melt the butter and coat both side of tortillas generously; then fill with chicken and cheese mixture and roll. Lay enchiladas in a pan, cover with cream and slices of Gruyere cheese and heat in moderately hot oven until lightly browned.

GREEN ENCHILADAS

24 tortillas	1 egg
3 medium bell peppers	1 cup peanut oil
⅓ lb. green tomatoes	½ lb. lean pork, roasted
2 medium onions	3 tbs. cream cheese
½ pt. cream	Cheddar cheese

Parboil the peppers and tomatoes, remove seeds from peppers, skin tomatoes, and grind together with onions in food chopper. Pour the cream into this green sauce and beat in the egg lightly.

Soak the tortillas in this mixture for ten minutes, then lightly fry each in hot oil until just pliable but not too hard. This may take a few minutes practice.

Fill the tortillas with shredded pork mixed with cream cheese, lay slices of cheddar on top, and pour on remaining green sauce. Heat in warm oven for five minutes or so.

Envueltos de Aguacate (AVOCADO WRAPAROUNDS)

18 tortillas	1 tbs. chili powder
4 tbs. chopped onion	6 average avocados
Peanut oil	Salt
2 cans tomato sauce	2 tbs. lime juice

Sauté two tablespoons of chopped onion in one tablespoon oil until soft but uncolored; stir in tomato sauce and chili and cook five minutes.

Mash the avocado meat to a uniform paste and stir in salt, two tablespoons chopped onion and lime juice.

In hot, deep cooking oil drop each tortilla, turning immediately and removing. Tortilla should brown lightly but remain soft.

Fill each tortilla with avocado sauce, double over and pour tomato dressing on top.

Serve from platter adorned with olives, radishes and sliced cheddar cheese.

Envueltos de Puré de Chícharos
(GREEN PEA WRAPAROUNDS)

18 small tortillas
2 cups thick pea purée

Sour cream
Peanut oil

Fry the tortillas in deep oil quickly, so they don't harden—then double. Fill them with hot pea purée or cream of pea soup that has been heated without adding water.

Lay the *envuelto* on a plate and spoon sour cream over top.

Garnachas con Frijoles Refritos

Garnachas are just the thing to serve the next time your friends come over to watch a football game on TV. Have a reefer full of cold beer, a big platter of *garnachas* and no one will talk during the close plays.

1 doz. tortillas
1 lb. lean beef in chunks
½ onion
½ green pepper
1 large tomato
Oil

Refried beans (see following recipe)
Powdered yellow cheese
Chopped green onions
Finely chopped lettuce

Boil the meat for an hour then put it through a food chopper with the onion, tomato and pepper; sauté until the pepper is tender. Cut the tortillas in quarters and brown in deep fat (commercial corn chips can be used).

Spread each one very lightly with refried beans, meat sauce, powdered cheese, chopped onions and lettuce. See next recipe for refried beans. Enough for six nervous football watchers.

Frijoles Refritos (REFRIED BEANS)

Refried beans is the friendliest dish in Mexico, it gets along famously with everybody and everything. *Refritos* shows up at breakfast with eggs and tortillas; at the second course of the *comida* it comes in brown and warm, and even during the stateliest dinner its benign presence is revealed.

Refritos must be made from the right bean or they are as off key as a Cossack singing the "Star Spangled Banner." There are close to a hundred varieties of beans in Mexico. I have counted twenty-five types in one market stall—but only three or four are used for *refritos*. The large Mexican Red, often sold in this country is absolutely top drawer; the pinto is used and so is the black. Kidney beans will serve in a pinch, but they are too mushy to give you the real McLopez.

Soak the beans overnight and put on to cook in the morning with a chopped onion and a ham hock or half a pound of chopped bacon. Don't add salt for three hours as the salt tends to harden the beans. When the beans are done, you are in business.

Give the frying pan medium heat and anoint it with two tablespoons of olive oil, peanut oil or bacon grease. Any one is excellent, but oil is better for the stomach. Ladle in the beans and mash them with a potato masher, sprinkle on Parmesan cheese liberally and keep mashing. If the *refritos* are too dry, pour in a tiny bit of bean soup. In ten minutes the noblest Mexican of them all will be ready for your pleasure.

Garnachas Colima

This is a lazy man's recipe which can be tossed in fifteen minutes. Quarter and fry the tortillas and spread thickly with *guacamole*.

Guacamole Colima

Guacamole is a versatile sauce that can be used over meat, fish or beans and as a spread or dip. There is no set way to prepare it; vary the ingredients to suit your own taste.

Send two big, preferably dead ripe avocados through the food chopper with one *chile verde* or half a bell pepper and a quarter of an onion. Mix in a tablespoon of lemon juice, a pinch of coriander, salt and pepper and chill. A tablespoon of mayonnaise and a dash of Worcestershire will make the *guacamole* dippier.

A *guacamole* with more zest is made by chopping and mixing

two avocados, four tomatoes, two piquant green peppers, one large onion, a pinch of coriander, salt and oil. Lemon juice or dry, white wine may be substituted for oil

Don't say I didn't warn you. The Mexicans claim that avocados are an aphrodisiac.

Gordas

Gorda means "fat girl" and the woman who showed me how to compose one in Cuernavaca was well cast for the part. She laughed constantly from sheer good spirits, and her plump body followed her patting hands in an undulating hula. She operated a four-seat booth in the market, and her clientele was made up of long time *aficionados* who dropped in for her personalized *gordas*, a few minutes of music from her radio and a spot of gossip.

She took a handful of *masa*, patted it into a large tortilla, put in a big spoonful of refried beans, wrapped the *masa* around the beans and repatted it into a *gorda* that looked like a pregnant pancake. She quickly fried the *gorda* in deep fat, pricked a hole in the middle with a fork, poured in a spoonful of sour cream and offered it with the majesty of a queen presenting a coronet.

Orejas de Cerdo a la Leonesa
(PIG'S EARS LEON STYLE)

This is an old time Spanish tid bit that has taken deep hold on the Mexican affection. Use only male ears for this delicacy and save the sow's ears for purses.

4 pig's ears	2 tbs. flour
1 onion chopped	1 qt. soup stock
Cooking oil	Salt and pepper

Cook the *orejas* in salted water until tender, approximately forty minutes.

Fry the onion in two spoons of olive or peanut oil and stir in the *orejas* cut in small pieces. Add flour and brown lightly; pour in the soup stock, salt and pepper; stir well and simmer fifteen minutes.

Serve with fried bread and lime to squeeze in the soup.

Pastas Pachuqueñas (PACHUCA STYLE MEAT TARTS)

Pachuca, capital of Hidalgo, sits in a deep canyon of the Eastern Sierra at an elevation of a mile and a half. Silver mines honeycomb the surrounding hills and smelters bubble day and night. Six miles up the mountain is the Real del Monte, which has produced millions of dollars in silver.

Ever since a Cornishman first entered a mine shaft, meat pasties have probably appeared in the lunch buckets of miners throughout most of the world. Mexico is no exception, and not the least of Pachuca's treasure is its *pastas*, savory and heartening enough for a miner on his way home from a shift in the shaft.

1 lb. tender round steak	2 tbs. chopped parsley
1 lb. potatoes	2 seeded and chopped
2 leeks	pickled peppers
3 cup recipe for biscuit dough	Salt

Make a *relleno* or filling by slicing meat in the thinnest possible strips, peeling and cutting potatoes shoestring style, and chopping the leeks with all but the tenderest layers removed. Keep potatoes in salted water until they are to be used.

Mix and roll out the biscuit dough about an eighth of an inch thick. Try this out once to get the exact thickness so the dough will bake at the same rate as the filling.

Cut out circles from the dough five inches in diameter, and fill with the meat, potatoes, leeks, parsley, and peppers, all lightly salted. Double the dough and crimp the edges. Swab with milk and bake uncovered in preheated 350° oven for twenty minutes. Test potatoes for doneness with a toothpick.

Serve with lots of guacamole and black coffee. Four servings.

Pisto (SPANISH OMELETTE)

In recreating Mexican foods, American cooks are constantly tempted to overdress simple but typical dishes, so the result is frequently as flamboyantly overdone as a Hollywood version of the Mexican hat dance.

Pisto is simple and dignified. It demands strict attention to the protocol of blending and heat regulation, but it wants no tampering with its ancient pedigree.

¼ lb. lean, uncooked ham	1 can tomato sauce
2 tbs. cooking oil	6 eggs
2 onions finely chopped	Salt
2 medium bell peppers, sliced	

Chop the ham in small squares and fry slowly in the oil; remove the ham to cool and sauté the onions and sliced peppers in the same oil. Add the tomato sauce and simmer until the onions and peppers are tender.

Break the eggs into a bowl, salt and add the ham. Stir lightly but don't whip. Add to the tomato recaudo and mix in quickly. Cook over a slow fire, moving the pan constantly for uniform heat and turn out as one omelette which is then divided into four portions.

Garnish each plate with sliced, hard-cooked eggs and freshly fried ham.

Quesadillas

Quesadillas are the chameleons of Mexican *antojitos*. They change their shape and makeup to conform to local taste and fancy. In the "synchronized *quesadilla*" two small tortillas are filled, sandwich style, fastened with toothpicks, and fried. In Vera Cruz one tortilla is filled, rolled like a cigar and called a *molote*, and in Nogales the rolled, meat-filled snack staggers under the name of *chimichanga*.

Fillings are as individual as the Mexican character. *Molotes* are stuffed with fried banana while a national favorite is a filling of chopped calf brains flavored with nutmeg. Perhaps the simplest and commonest *quesadilla* is wrapped around thin slices of cheese and *raja*. *Raja* is made by frying a chopped onion with strips of dry *chile ancho*, but a spoon of chili powder will do the same job as the broad pepper. The boiled, white cheese of Oaxaca is considered the number one *queso* of the country.

I made the acquaintance of my favorite *quesadillas* in lovely Uruapan, high in the mountains of Michoacan. Here the food sellers set up at dark beneath the arcades and prepare their savory viands under the light of kerosene lamps. Uruapan is famous for *corunda*—tamales in *mole* sauce—but I award the blue ribbon to *quesadillas con picadillo*.

1 lb. masa	½ cup corn starch
1 tbs. salt	4 tbs. peanut oil
½ cup milk	

Mix the masa, salt, milk and corn starch thoroughly and let it stand an hour. Pat out tortillas about four inches across and fry in oil. Cover each tortilla with picadillo in following recipe, fold over and pinch edges together. Fry quickly either in deep fat or in a completely dry skillet, according to taste.

Picadillo

½ lb. ground round	1 tbs. chopped parsley
½ lb. lean pork sausage	18 seedless raisins
1 tbs. chopped onion	18 almonds
1 can tomato paste	

To make the *picadillo*, sauté the onions and crumbled meat until the meat is well browned. Add the tomato paste and cook ten minutes over slow heat, put in the parsley, raisins and thinly sliced almonds, and cook another ten minutes.

Sopes (So-pays)

Food and fiestas in Mexico are as inseparable as peanuts and parties in this country, and the little *sope* modestly follows the Holy Day circuit.

My happiest memory of the *sope* is in Mazanillo. The Virgin of Guadalupe is the patron saint of the church, and the townsfolk celebrate from December 1 to the 12th. Each evening at dusk when the church services are over, the costumed dancers perform *La Conquista* in the street which fronts the church, and the ladies of the Church Guild sell food and drink to raise money for their poor box.

An open-air pavilion covered with palm branches takes over another part of the street, and the ladies dispense soft drinks and beer, *atole*, *pozole*, tamales and *sopes*. It is an enchanting experience to sit at a wooden table and enjoy the savory food while the nose is titillated by the smell of charcoal fires and steaming pots and the ear is haunted with the skirling chirimía and throbbing deer skin drums.

Sopes are simply made. Either pat out a three inch tortilla or trim down a ready-made tortilla with a pair of scissors. Fry quickly in fat, so the *sope* is light gold in color but not hard, and cover with chopped, crisp cabbage. Over this spoon a thin layer of crumbled hamburger and chili powder that has been slowly fried in a covered pan, surmount with finely chopped onion and cover with shredded cheese.

Serve each guest a cold bottle of beer and provide a bowl of fresh *salsa* made by grinding two ripe tomatoes, an onion and two piquant green peppers—or a sweet pepper and a sprinkle of cayenne—and salt.

Tacos

A taco is the simplest *antojito* to make. One simply puts whatever is handy into the doubled and fried tortilla. I have seen Mexicans stuff a taco with rice, beans, crumbled chorizo, shredded chicken or stewed goat. In Tehuantepec a gourmet finds tacos filled with delicate iguana meat; Tampico is noted for armadillo tacos, and the hardy mountaineers in the state of Hidalgo use the maguey worm to complement their *tacos de gusano*.

The best tacos I found in Mexico were in Perote. Perote sits on a wide plain a mile and a half above sea level on the highway between Puebla and Vera Cruz. Another highway turns northward and seeks the Gulf at Tecolutla. Buses and cars make a leisurely stop here, and people eat tacos while they stretch their legs.

A brisk, friendly woman served me two tacos; then as happily shared her *modus de operandi*. As usual I have taken a few liberties with the basic formula before bringing it across the border. The following should fill about one dozen tortillas.

1 onion, chopped	2 solid pack tomatoes, drained
½ green pepper	Salt and pepper
1 tbs. bacon fat	1 head lettuce, shredded
1 lb. ground round, lean	Small bowl grated
½ raw potato grated into meat	sharp cheese
1 can tomato sauce	Small bowl fresh salsa
1 tsp. chili powder	1 cup peanut oil

Sauté the chopped onion and green pepper in bacon fat until they are limp then add meat and potato mixed and crumbled. Brown for five minutes and pour in tomato sauce, tomatoes, chili powder, salt and pepper. Simmer over low heat for two hours until meat is crumbly and fairly dry. Don't hurry this bit; the filling is the taco.

Just before you are ready to serve, prepare bowls of shredded lettuce, grated cheese and *salsa*.

Double tortillas, put in meat filling, hold with tongs and fry quickly in hot oil. The taco should be golden and slightly firm but not hard. Drain on paper napkins and allow each guest to continue building. Ordinarily one puts tomato or *salsa* on next, then lettuce and sprinkles cheese over the whole thing.

If your friends are old Mexico hands, have a bottle of hot sauce standing by.

Tamales

The small Mexican tamales, about three fingers in thickness, can be bought in cans at most markets, however, the big, fat Texas tamales are most often used in the United States.

We are used to chicken and beef tamales, but in the southern Republic a bit of dedicated research will turn up shrimp, rabbit, deer, squash flower, fish, bean and cheese tamales. My favorite tamale stop is on the West Coast Highway where it crosses the Santiago River a thousand miles south of the border. Here the buses make a half hour layover and children vend oranges and bananas as well as steaming hot chicken, pork and shrimp tamales.

If you don't care to open cans, here is the basic routine for tamale rolling. Whip together a pound of corn *masa* with half a pound of lard (use lard rather than oil to get the authentic flavor) —until the *masa* is fluffy and a spoonful will float in water. Have a stack of corn shucks that have been soaked for half an hour in water and drained. Spread *masa* half an inch thick on a shuck, cover with filling and roll up. Wrap the *tamal* in four thicknesses of shucks, tie ends securely and cook for an hour in a tightly closed steamer above boiling water.

To make a filling, sauté a garlic clove, half an onion, two small green or wax peppers and a pound of finely chopped, cooked pork, beef or chicken. Pour in a can of tomato sauce and simmer until *relleno* thickens.

Tinga Poblana

Mole poblano left home to roam the Republic, but its modest cousin *tinga* remained in Puebla where everybody knows and adores her. She is delicate and demure, but, should you meet her in one of the many excellent cafes near the old, tree-filled plaza, you will find her saucy, piquant and satisfyingly lusty.

1 tender stewing chicken	2 cans tomato sauce
1 small onion	1 cup broth
2 cloves garlic	3 *chiles chilpotle* or any green
1 tbs. parsley	peppers in vinegar
1 tbs. oil	Salt and pepper

Cut the chicken in serving size pieces and put on to cook in a minimum amount of water with salt and pepper.

Chop the onion, garlic and parsley and sauté lightly in oil, then add chopped tomatoes or tomato sauce and simmer five minutes. When the chicken is almost done, add it to the *recaudo* with one cup broth and cook slowly until the meat is done. Clean and slice the green peppers and stir into the *tinga* and cook a few minutes longer. The *tinga* should be the same consistency as fricassee. In Puebla it is served straight, garnished with lettuce and sliced avocados; however, should you wish to remove the bones and serve it over toast and sprinkle paprika on top, no one will report you. Approximately four.

Tortitas de Camote (SWEET POTATO FRITTERS)

2 lbs. cooked sweet potatoes	2 tbs. flour
1 cup *picadillo* (see recipe)	Cooking oil
3 eggs, separated	Salt and pepper

Peel and slice sweet potatoes about half an inch thick. Put *picadillo* between pairs of slices to form sandwiches and fasten with half toothpicks.

Beat the egg yolks with flour and whip the whites until stiff; combine yolks and whites, add salt and pepper and continue beating until smooth.

Dip the *tortitas* in this batter and fry.

Tortitas de Carne (MEAT PATTY SURPRISE)

12 seedless raisins	¼ cup tomato paste
12 almonds	5 tbs. bread crumbs
6 black olives	1 ½ lbs. leftover roast beef
1 tbs. cooking oil	2 eggs
1 tsp. chopped onion	Salt and pepper
1 tsp. chopped parsley	

Soak raisins and almonds an hour; blanch, peel and grind almonds. Pit and chop olives fine.

Heat the oil and sauté onion then add parsley, tomato paste and bread crumbs. Cook five minutes and remove from heat.

Add meat which has gone through food chopper, beaten eggs, almonds, raisins and olives. Salt and pepper and stir thoroughly then form into patties.

Dip patties in batter and fry.

FRITURA BATTER

2 eggs, separated	½ cup oil
1 tbs. flour	

Beat the egg whites until stiff, add yolks and continue until uniform. Stir in the flour.

Serve the *tortitas* with green salad and green *salsa*.

Drinks

Drinks

A BEAKER OF THE WARM SOUTH

O for a beaker full of the warm South!
Full of the true, the blushful Hippocrene,
With beaded bubbles winking at the brim,
    And purple stained mouth;
That I might drink, and leave the world unseen,
And with thee fade away into the forest dim:
                    JOHN KEATS. *"Ode to a Nightingale."*

IN THE DAYS of antiquity when gods walked the beautiful land of Mexico, a lovely and generous lady passed through the country. The lady's name was Mayahuel, and she was goddess of maguey. She had searched the entire world for a land and a people worthy of her precious gift.

That gift was the *agave* plant, a succulent which provides fiber for twine, mats and clothes, as well as needle and thread to fabricate them. Best of all, however, the sap can be fermented for *pulque* or distilled into *tequila*.

Mayahuel liked the high, golden slopes and the friendly people, so she scattered her blue-green maguey plants from the northern deserts to the jungles of Yucatan.

Centuries later the husband of Mayahuel, Tepotztecatl, God of Octli, returned to Mexico and taught the people to make *octli* by the simple process of fermenting maguey sap. Still more centuries passed before the Spaniards came and imported the name *pulque* from Chile. Today both gods have been chased from the land by the Spanish fathers, but millions of acres of *maguey* are alembicated into *tequila, mescal, charanda* and *sotol*.

The heart land for tequila brewing is in Jalisco, where the light green fields of *maguey* look like an arm of the sea. The town of

Tequila, thirty miles west of Guadalajara, has nearly a dozen distilleries which turn out most of the *tequila* produced. The *fabrica* of Jose Cuervo is the biggest, and his product the most popular in Mexico.

It has been the custom for most American writers to refer to *tequila* as a "fiery liquor," without doing any apparent field research. Actually *tequila* is the same proof as a mild brandy. *Cuervo tequila*, sold in the United States, is 86 proof. Its noteworthy feature, aside from its versatility, is its marked lack of hangover. North Americans have been assiduous in refusing to buy *tequila* while in Mexico for eighty cents a quart, but it is becoming quite smart to pay six dollars a fifth in the United States.

The classical way to sip *tequila* is to sprinkle salt on the wrist, toss it in the mouth, take a swallow of *tequila*, and chase it with a bite of lime or lemon. This custom has been euphemized into the mixed drink called a Margarita.

Charanda is another form of *tequila* made from the *maguey* local to Uruapan. *Mescal* is distilled from the blue-green plants of Oaxaca. In Tlacolula, twenty-five miles south of the state capital, the discriminating traveller can buy *mescal* from the factories that feature the typically regional squat, black pottery bottles.

Sotol is made in the Chihuahua desert from the narrow bladed, pale green maguey, and sold only in the area.

An etymological sidelight on Mexico is that distilleries are *fabricas*, or factories, and that one does not drink beverages, he takes them. To sample food or drink is to prove it. Thus the publican will offer a small glass and say *"pruebelo."*

Pulque is a milky liquid which is dispensed in *pulquerías* from open barrels. On the old haciendas the workers receive part of their pay in *pulque*, half a gallon a day being the usual dole for a laborer. Everybody from babies to grandmothers eagerly sup all they can get.

Social workers took a dim view of the national custom, but they were confounded when dieticians discovered that *pulque* was one of the highest known sources of vitamins. The government maintains a tax on every *maguey* plant and attempts to cut down on production and consumption of *pulque*, but every night the *pulquería's* rafters rock to the old refrain:

Oh, know ye that *pulque* is liquor divine;
The Angels in Heaven prefer it to wine.

MEXICAN WINE, RUM, BRANDY AND CORDIALS

The Spaniards forbade wine growing in Mexico. Naturally— they wanted another eager market for Spanish wines. It was not until around 1600 that the first vines were smuggled into Parras and Coahuila, where the Marqués de Aguayo, who was far enough away from the capital to do pretty well what he pleased, started grape squeezing.

Today, Parras of the Fountain is a picturesque little oasis in the northern desert flaunting wide acres of Pinot Noir and Palomino grapes, and half a dozen wineries. The Aguayo winery claims 1590 as its founding date, and the Madero *fábrica* posts 1620 as its birth. Both admit to be the original plant founded. Incidentally, President Francisco I. Madero, a member of the vintner clan, was born in Parras.

Probably as a result of this *vino* veto Mexico has only three wine producing centers: Parras, Aguascalientes and Santo Tomás in Baja California. Mexico's Central Highway passes by the extensive vineyards and large *bodegas* of the wine makers a few miles north of the city of Aguascalientes. The altitude is a mile high and the soil is a sandy silt.

Santo Tomás lies in a wide river valley twenty five miles from the Pacific. The soil is similar to that of Graves, France. The rocks of a deep gravel reef reflect heat into the vines and produce remarkably fine grapes. *Bodegas* Santo Tomás are located in the town of Ensenada twenty miles to the north.

Nowhere else is the extreme individuality of the Mexican shown better than in his wine trampling; one might say there is the right way, the wrong way, and the Mexican way.

In Aguascalientes I talked with a wine master who had never heard of the Cabernet Sauvignon, Pinot Noir or Gamay grapes, the standard berry for producing Bordeaux, Burgundy or most other red wines. Nevertheless this *bodega* gleefully turned out red and white table wines, Ports and Sherries from twenty-five kinds of table grapes, the most common of which were Ribier and Thompson Seedless.

The Parras and Santo Tomas wineries stick pretty close to standard European grapes, so excellent wines and brandies can be found in their dozens of generic and varietal offerings.

About the only way to find a Mexican wine for one's taste is through the exciting and rewarding game of tasting. It is estimated that nearly a million Americans visit Mexico each year, and ninety per cent of them don't know what to do once they are established. What better hobby for a lonely tourist than to set up his own wine tasting service? He will soon find the country is full of friends.

The most worthwhile research I have ever done, as far as advancing the betterment of mankind, was combing the back country of Mexico for individually made fruit wines. One gets leads in the most obscure and fascinating ways: a sentence in an old book, a Mexican friend who casually mentions his boyhood village, or a note in a tourist bulletin pointing up the picturesque in a little visited region.

At Atotonilco el Alto, in the highlands of Jalisco, is the Rojas *Fábrica* which makes a mellow, golden orange wine. It is one of life's high spots to sit in a cafe fronting the plaza and watch the horse and mule pack trains trudge past, loaded with produce from the mountains, and to savor this rich-bodied *vino de naranja*.

Ixtlahuacán sits just off the Guadalajara-Chapala Highway. The woman who runs a general store on the plaza sells her own ruby colored quince wines. She washes up tequila bottles, fills and corks them, but doesn't bother to replace the label. The superb character of this *vino de membrillo* rises Cinderella-like above its humble surroundings.

In the soaring Eastern Sierra, Acaxochitlán, at an elevation of 8100 feet, is the center of extensive fruit orchards. The town is a few miles south of Tulancingo and specializes in fruit wines. For thirty-two cents I bought a liter of lilting apple champagne; however a bottle of the rare and tangy *acachul*, wild grape wine, set me back forty-eight cents.

Assessing the wines in a Mexican liquor or grocery store is as breathtaking as inventorying the *houris* in a recently auctioned harem. Here is a dark red wine called "Blood of Christ"; and it turns out to be sweet-sour and fruity. This pale yellow package is aptly named "Tears of the Virgin"; it is delicate of body but slightly woody from long weeping in an oaken cask.

Yonder is a sherry which humbly states: "Dry Pallid." This one is indeed dry, with the unmistakable aroma of muscat grapes. A beautifully carved bottle attracts the eye, and the label reads "Jerez Quemada"—Burned Sherry. This wine was fabricated in Guadalajara where wine is made from raisins, a practice common in Puebla and the Capital. Sure enough, it has a bitter aftertaste. Probably an apprentice let the liquid get low in the vats and a thrifty winemaster renamed the batch.

A wine so red it is almost black, hides behind a "White Cross Port" name plate. This *vino* has vigorous body and excellent taste; one sip betrays the aroma of blackberries. It is not Port, but who cares. It is gorgeous. The last bottle on the day's sampling is from Parras and is honestly labelled, "Málaga." It is a rich Burgundy red and rewards us with a full, but not fat body, and a lovely, untampered savor.

On the surface it might seem an expensive hobby to find only two excellent wines out of six tries, but then the bottles only cost from fifty to seventy cents each.

Mexico produces some excellent brandies, even though the vintners and dealers have a near schizophrenia over what to call them. For years brandy was called *coñac*, but France has kept heckling other countries not to let the name cognac be used for anything but brandy from the Cognac region.

As a consequence Mexico forbids the use of the name *coñac*, and the bottles are labeled brandy, brondy (which doesn't catch on) aguardiente, or Parras.

The *fábricas* of Aguayon and Madero have been creating good brandies for 450 years in Parras, and in the *fábrica* Delfin for a somewhat shorter time. Madero XXXXX is a brandy without breeding which is perhaps best known to Mexicans and Americans. Santo Tomás makes good brandy, and the producers in Aguascalientes turn out several passable labels.

All three wine and brandy centers can be reached by car on paved roads, and it is one of the pleasures of touring Mexico to visit the *fábricas*.

Rum is the golden essence of sunshine distilled from tropical sugar cane. *Ron* is the standard name for rum; *cachupe* is a strong liquor made from cane and can scarcely be classed as a rum, while *habañero* is top grade. *Habañero añejo* is aged rum, and the word *añejo* alone is a proud name with either liquor or cheese.

All Mexican rums are good, from the humble *Berreteaga*, sold all over Mexico in its red, white and green package for about sixty cents a bottle, to the best grades which command about five dollars for a wicker-covered gallon.

Anyone travelling the Pan-American Highway south of Laredo can see the entire rum-making cycle. On both sides of the highway are thousands of acres of growing cane, and in Mante is the largest sugar mill, or "engine," as the Mexicans call it. Ten miles south of Valles and facing the pavement is the fine, modern Huasteca rum *fábrica*.

The most picturesque and fascinating of Mexico's industries is the fruit wine and fruit liqueur fabrication. In dozens of out-of-the-way villages are one family plants which have been turning out orange, quince or apple wine for generations. Generally they are fiercely proud of their product, which is all hand-done from the picking and squeezing to the stoppering.

The undisputed cordial center of Mexico, where probably ninety per cent of her *licores* are produced is Tenancingo. Tenancingo is on a secondary paved highway between Toluca and Taxco, at an elevation of a mile and a half. Five ancient *fábricas* each turn out forty five different fruit *licores* and sell them locally at sixty cents a liter. A liter is slightly more than a quart.

Making a cordial is simplicity itself. The fruit—which may be apple, blackberry, quince, mint, banana or any of forty others—is pressed, and both juice and pulp is poured into an open barrel. Enough alcohol is added to cover the *maceración* and allowed to stand eight days.

The *maceración* is then strained through linen bags into other casks, and half as much simple syrup and half as much alcohol is added. The liquor in the cask is now called *infusión*. It is fined to precipitate sediment and allowed to stand exactly thirty two days to clarify completely.

Tenancingo is a gracious old town which seldom sees a tourist. It is a *reboza* weaving center, and at the Sunday market hundreds of the hand-woven scarves, each different, are displayed. This is the gateway to Chalma, the miracle working shrine, and it is the one place in the world where every man who wears shoes is an expert in blending cordials.

We are timidly learning to accept the Grasshopper and a few other blended cordial drinks, but it will be long ere we can boldly toss in a dollop from a blue *crema*, then drip in yellow and green, and lace the creation with vermillion, as do the masters in Tenancingo.

Rompope is a sort of egg nog base that is produced in Tenancingo and made famous under the arcades in Morelia. It is spooned up by women and children like ice cream, and mixed with brandy by the men.

Should you care to make a batch for an important anniversary, here's how.

Rompope

2 qts. milk
2 lbs. sugar
  Sprinkle cinnamon, nutmeg
  and clove

¾ qt. alcohol (1½ qts. if using
  100 proof rum and add a tsp.
  vanilla)
10 egg yolks

Boil the milk, sugar and spices until thick. Remove from fire. When cool, skim and add alcohol very slowly. Beat the eggs until thick and then add to milk slowly, beating constantly.

Cóctel Bandera Mexicana
(MEXICAN FLAG COCKTAIL)

½ pt. *tequila*
  Juice of 2½ limes
3 tbs. powdered sugar

1 banana, Thompson seedless
  grapes and maraschino
  cherries

Mix the sugar and lime juice thoroughly, and then pour in *tequila*. Shake with chopped ice and serve in cocktail glasses.

Into each glass drop a grape, cherry and banana ball to flaunt the red, white and green of the Mexican flag.

Cuernavaca Cooler

This cooler is the friend of tropical loungers, lovers and beach-combers. It makes a delightful party punch.

4 pts. sweet white wine
1 pt. sweet red wine
1 pt. *tequila*
1 pt. rum

3 oranges cut in wheels
2 apples, cored and sliced thin
Sugar to taste
Ice

Pour all ingredients in large punch bowl with ice. Add sugar slowly and savor until perfect taste is reached. This is the most fun, because you may have to sip five or six samples before it is just right.

La Tuna (THE PRICKLY PEAR)

Here is a West Coast favorite. Serve it with cooked, hulled shrimp and seafood dip.

4 dashes bitters
1 jigger *tequila*
1 tsp. lime juice

Club soda
Salt

Use an Old Fashion glass and fill with ice cubes. Pour in tequila, bitters, lime juice and soda. Sprinkle salt on top of ice cubes.

Margarita

This is good for that enchanted evening when you have met a beautiful stranger and wish to thaw some ice together.

1 oz. *tequila*
1 oz. lime or lemon juice

½ oz. triple sec

Shake with cracked ice. Moisten rim of the glass with lime juice and rub in salt sprinkled on napkin. Fill glass and drink over the salted edge.

Nube Nueve (CLOUD NINE)

This is particularly good if you are suspicious of the water in a region. Observe that none is necessary. The nutrient effect from the egg and the vitamins in the fruit fortifies one for a long, lazy ride on his cloud.

1 oz. *tequila*	1 egg, beaten
1 oz. brandy	Sprig of mint
Juice two limes	

Create the same as for "Tequila Dream" and garnish with mint. Happy landings!

Rosita Borrachita (ROSIE THE DRUNKARDESS)

1 jigger grenadine	2 tsps. lime juice
3 jiggers *tequila*	

Shake well with ice and strain into glasses.

Sangrita de Chapala

Sangrita has been mixed in Chapala for years. It was served cold as an apéritif or *entremets*. Some daring soul decided *sangrita* had a natural affinity for *tequila*, and visitors spread the word to the corners of the Republic.

When the gringos discovered *sangrita* and *tequila*, the fame of *sangrita* skyrocketed. *Sangrita de la Viuda* is a trade name, and the blenders have their own formula which is packaged and sold in Mexico and the United States.

Here is the nonsecret formula from Chapala.

½ pt. orange juice	½ tsp. hot sauce
3 tbs. grenadine syrup	1 tbs. salt

Shake well and chill. *Sangrita* is sipped after each swallow of tequila by some, while others mix one part *tequila* to four parts *sangrita* to make a cocktail.

Señorita

4 jiggers *tequila*	3 jiggers Curaçao
4 jiggers lime juice	

Moisten the rim of a long stemmed goblet by rubbing with lime; twirl in salt to coat rim of glass.

Shake the ingredients with cracked ice and serve. Six servings.

Tequila Dream (OR JARABE TAPATIO)

Juice of three limes
1 oz. grenadine
1 egg, beaten

1 oz. *tequila*
Maraschino cherry

Put the lime juice in shaker and add the grenadine blended with the egg; move slowly until ingredients incorporate. Add *tequila* and cracked ice and shake well. Serve with a maraschino cherry.

Bamboo

½ sherry
½ sweet Vermouth

Dash Angostura bitters

Shake with ice and strain into glass.

Beachcomber

1 ½ jiggers light rum
½ jigger Cointreau

Juice of half a lime
2 dashes Maraschino liqueur

Shake with cracked ice and serve.

Bitter Batido

Angostura bitters has been compounded for almost a hundred and fifty years in the Caribbean area. It is widely used in soups and sauces; it is also ladled up as a medicine to ward off the miseries. *Bitter batido* is simply beaten bitters, but think what it can do for you on a foggy night.

I am particularly fond of this mix because it is the private creation of a Peruvian Admiral who gave it to me in Lima.

1 jigger sweet Vermouth
1 jigger bitters

White of an egg

Beat thoroughly with fine ice and serve in liqueur glasses.

Bolo Cocktail

A bolo is a sharp knife used for cane cutting or head hunting. If you should care to cut a wide swath, try two or three.

2 jiggers Bacardi
Juice ½ lime

Juice ¼ orange
Spoonful powdered sugar

Shake with cracked ice and serve.

Bongo Punch

¼ sherry
¼ port

¼ Curaçao
¼ soda water

Mix sherry, port and Cuaraçao in punch bowl with ice; add soda just before serving and garnish with orange slices.

Bosom Caresser

⅔ jigger brandy
⅓ jigger Curaçao

1 tsp. grenadine
1 egg yolk

Shake thoroughly with ice and strain into glass.

Brandy and Bitters

3 jiggers brandy
½ jigger Curaçao
½ tsp. bitters
Pinch nutmeg

Tsp. grated lemon rind
1 egg, beaten
Sugar

Beat all ingredients except the sugar thoroughly, then lovingly add sugar and taste until it gets there.

Chicha

Chicha is a native drink that has been compounded for five hundred or more years along the Caribbean coast from Mexico to

South America. Today in Panama the word "*chicha*" is used for any drink, even orange juice is *chicha de naranja.*

The women of a tribe chewed corn kernels until they filled an *olla* with the masticated *masa.* It then stood for three days, at which time it was ready for a marriage feast. Today the Indians of Yucatán, Honduras and the San Blas Indians of Panama still celebrate with corn *chicha.*

However here is the polite *chicha* which serves for a gentle refreshment.

1 large pineapple	6 limes
4 qts. water	¼ tsp. each cinnamon, cloves,
2 lbs. sugar	nutmeg

Peel the pineapple and cut the peel into small sections; mash the pulp. Dissolve the sugar in water; add the limes sliced and all other ingredients.

Let it stand one or two days in a clay vessel or crock until the *chicha* takes on a sharp, hard cider taste. Strain, ice and serve.

Crema de Café

1 pt. vodka
4 cups sugar
4 cups water
¾ cup instant coffee
1 ½ oz. pure vanilla

Bring water to a boil. Add instant coffee and dissolve thoroughly. Add sugar and simmer for 10 minutes.

Remove from fire and add vanilla. Let cool to tepid and add vodka. Mix thoroughly and bottle. Can be drunk immediately, but improves with age.

Cuba Libre

The *Cuba Libre* is probably the best known drink in the American tropics. The name means Free Cuba and was the slogan of the Cubans in the time of Teddy Roosevelt. When the message was carried to Garcia, it was probably the recipe for this drink.

1 ½ jiggers rum   Any cola drink
  Juice of half a lime

Put the rum and lime juice in a highball glass, add two ice cubes and fill the glass with cola.

Curaçao Punch

1 jigger rum   ½ tsp. sugar
1 jigger Curaçao   Juice ½ lemon

Stir in a large glass and fill with shaved ice; stir once more lightly. Decorate with half an orange slice.

Daiquiri

This drink is as much at home in the entire Caribbean as the hurricane. It is primarily a Cuban drink made with Bacardi.

1 jigger rum   Juice one lime
2 dashes grenadine

Shake well with cracked ice and strain or fill glass with finely chopped ice and pour in drink for a frappé.

Diablo

6 jiggers brandy   1 tsp. Angostura bitters
6 jiggers dry Vermouth   2 tsps. orange bitters

Shake with ice and strain into glasses. Serve with lemon peel or cherries to six.

El Presidente

Mexico's aristocrat of drinks is loved by all true *aficionados*.

It is likely called "The President" because it is of high quality, lasts such a short time and leaves its supporters half shot.

1 jigger light rum
½ oz. Vermouth

2 dashes grenadine
Juice ½ lime

Shake with ice and serve for a short term.

El Suspiro (THE SIGHBALL)

1 jigger rum
1 jigger creme de cacao

1 jigger dry Vermouth
2 drops peppermint

Shake well with cracked ice, adorn with cherry, and drink with a sigh.

Firefly

⅔ light rum
⅓ brandy

1 tsp. lemon juice
1 tsp. grenadine

Stir with ice and strain.

Golden Island Cocktail

Curaçao is an island in the southern Caribbean. It is also the name of a liqueur made of orange rind. Either way it spells tropical warmth and a perfect running mate for rum.

2 jiggers rum
2 tbs. Curaçao

Juice ½ lime

Shake with cracked ice and serve.

Granada Cocktail (POMEGRANATE COCKTAIL)

2 jiggers rum
2 jiggers pineapple juice

1 tsp. grenadine
Juice half a lime

Shake with cracked ice and strain into glasses.

Gulf Grog

Grog was invented in the British Navy to spread the supply. It was rum cut with water. Undoubtedly this drink filtered into Mexico almost 400 years ago when English pirates entertained the local girls on the beach.

1 wine glass rum	2 egg whites
½ pt. water	Juice 1 lime or ½ lemon
4 tbs. sugar	

Bring the water, sugar and lime juice to a boil. Beat the egg whites and stir into the rum.

With the water just under a boil add rum. Serve very hot.

Havana

1 jigger light rum	¼ jigger lemon juice
⅔ jigger pineapple juice	

Shake with ice and strain into glasses.

Jalapa Punch

Grated peel of 2 lemons	1 pt. applejack
2 ½ qts. hot black tea	1 pt. rum
1 pt. sugar syrup	1 pt. port

Drop grated lemon in punch bowl and pour hot tea in; let stand fifteen minutes and add syrup.

When it cools add the rest of the ingredients. Just before serving add a block of ice and thinly sliced lemon rounds.

Jalisco Hot Punch

Next Christmas if you tire of serving Tom and Jerrys, you might shake up your guests by displaying this heart warming wassail bowl.

1 pt. rum	1 jigger Curaçao or Triple
½ pt. brandy	Sec
2½ pts. black tea	6 tbs. powdered sugar
2½ pts. orange leaf tea (boil	Juice 1 lime
15 green orange leaves	
in 3 pts. water and	
strain)	

Warm the punchbowl thoroughly but carefully. Pour in the rum and brandy; add the other ingredients at a low boil, stir and pour while it's hot.

Jungle Juice

2 jiggers rum	1 tsp. orange juice
1 jigger Curaçao	1 tsp. lemon juice
1 tsp. pineapple juice	1 tsp. grenadine

Shake with ice and strain into glass.

La Guapita Coctail
(THE PRETTY LITTLE GIRL COCKTAIL)

The Pretty Little Girl is a favorite of Tenancingo. As any *bon vivant* knows, she is only to be savored after a gracious dinner.

1½ tbs. port wine	1 jigger creme de menthe
3 tbs. creme de cacao	1 jigger brandy
2 jiggers Curaçao	

Shake thoroughly with ice and serve in cocktail glasses with very thin slices of lemon on a toothpick.

Limonada Garrapiñada
(ICED LEMONADE LIQUEUR)

This is a Biscayan punch that is always served with codfish Biscayan style. If you and your guests are short of codfish, wink at tradition while the *garrafa* is being passed.

2 qts. white wine	1 pt. water (choose carefully)
1 pt. sherry	1 lb. bar sugar
½ pt. brandy	6 lemons or limes

Dissolve the sugar thoroughly in water, add the wine and brandy, then drop in the citrus cut in thin wheels. Chill until the pitcher or *garrafa* is frosted.

Mango

A *mango* is a flavorsome tropical fruit with a yellow skin and red cheeks. In Mexico "mango" is slang for looking particularly good or "sharp."

This cocktail is *muy mango*.

3 jiggers rum	1 jigger lime or lemon juice
1 jigger anisette	1 jigger grenadine

Shake well with ice cube and strain into glass. For two.

Mocambo Mixer

5 jiggers Curaçao	1 jigger rum
5 jiggers orange juice	Bitters
1 jigger brandy	

Barely coat inside of each glass with bitters; mix Curaçao, orange juice, brandy and rum with ice; shake well and strain into glasses.

Serves six unless everyone wants doubles, in which case, serves three.

Omar Cocktail

An Alexander can be made with either gin or brandy, but your true Mexican wants no half measures, so he puts in both. This drink fits the Old Tentmaker's admonition:

> "Come, take the cup that clears
> Today of past regrets and future fears."

1 jigger creme de cacao 1 jigger brandy
1 jigger gin 1 jigger fresh cream

Shake thoroughly with chopped ice and serve with a maraschino cherry.

Palmetto

½ St. Croix or West Indies rum 2 dashes orange bitters
½ sweet Vermouth

Stir with ice and strain into glasses. Serve with twist of lemon peel.

Planters Punch

This drink contains the smack of a tropical sunset, the music and the dancing. When you compose this punch wear a planter's straw hat to help you capture the intangibles.

3 jiggers rum 1 tsp. pineapple juice
  Juice two limes 1 tbs. grenadine
  Juice ¼ orange

Fill a highball glass with finely chopped ice and frost. Pour in ingredients and mix. Decorate glass with slices of orange, pineapple, cherry and mint.

Ponche Jardín (GARDEN PUNCH)

Garden Punch is just the thing to serve when the ladies of the Garden Club meet in your patio. The healthful fruits and natural juices will enhance their complexion and sharpen their creative imaginations.

4 fifths white dry wine ½ lb. small, fresh strawberries
2 fifths apple champagne or 12 maraschino cherries
  cider with a spike in it 3 oranges finely chopped
2 wine glasses brandy Sugar to taste
1 pt. soda water Ice
2 apples chopped fine

Mix slowly and start the countdown.

Rosemary Cocktail

While the men take their stronger drinks, the ladies daintily sip nectars tempered to their more delicate natures. Rosemary is woman's drink.

1 jigger Curaçao	4 jiggers mineral or soda water
1 jigger creme de menthe	3 tbs. powdered sugar
Juice of 1 lime or ½ lemon	

Shake long and lovingly with cracked ice so part will melt into the mix. Pour into large glasses and fill with soda water. Serve a thin lemon wheel on a toothpick in each glass. Recipe makes one drink.

Rum Cow

This is some of the hair off the dog. Try it to settle your stomach if you have had some bad water.

1 jigger rum	1 dash Angostura bitters
2 drops vanilla	2 tsp. sugar
1 cup milk	Pinch nutmeg

Shake well with ice and pour into a tall glass.

Rum Pot

½ jigger rum	3 dashes Angostura bitters
½ jigger port	1 jigger Curaçao
1 jigger brandy	

Shake with ice and strain into glass.

Sangría

1 jigger lime juice	1 pt. dry red wine
8 cups orange juice	

Mix with a spoon but don't shake. Serve in a tall glass full of chopped ice and garnish with a sprig of mint. Good for a summer afternoon.

Sevilla

Here is an interesting switcheroo—a mild, tropical Martini.

4 jiggers dry sherry   2 jiggers dry Vermouth
7 drops orange bitters

Shake well with ice and serve with a green olive on a toothpick. For two.

Sonora

½ Bacardi rum   ½ tsp. apricot brandy per drink
½ apple brandy   Splash lemon juice per drink

Stir with ice and strain into glasses.

Spanish Town

1 jigger rum   2 dashes Curaçao

Shake with ice and strain into glass. Sprinkle a bit of nutmeg on top.

Tenancingo Tango

This is a good drink for the high altitude where one should cut down on liquor consumption; it takes longer to get to the rum.

1 ½ jiggers rum   ½ jigger Anisette
½ jigger green creme   1 tbs. powdered sugar
    de menthe   2 jiggers mineral or soda water
1 ½ jiggers Curaçao

Shake with ice an extra long time (heavy liquors blend slowly) and serve in brandy glasses.

Tepache

Tepache is a remarkably crisp and refreshing drink that is known in all parts of Mexico. It is usually encountered only at fairs and fiestas, but in Cuernavaca it is dispensed daily in the plaza.

1 large pineapple
1 lb. barley
3 lbs. brown sugar

1 large piece cinnamon bark
8 whole cloves
Water

Crush the pineapple, hull and all, and cover with three quarts of water in a clay pot or crock; add the cinnamon and cloves and allow to stand two days.

On the second day boil the barley and sugar in a quart of water until the cereal swells and cracks. Add the barley water to the pineapple mash and let stand another two days.

Strain well and pour over a block of ice in a punch bowl and serve.

Trinidad

1 ½ jiggers Trinidad Rum
Juice ½ lime

1 tsp. powdered sugar
3 dashes Angostura bitters

Shake with ice and strain into glass.

Tropical

⅓ dry Vermouth
⅓ maraschino liquer
⅓ creme de cacao

1 dash orange bitters
1 dash Angostura bitters

Stir with ice and strain into glass.

Tropical Surprise Cocktail

This is a basic rum recipe. It is great with any rum, but it will take its character from the rum used.

Wine glass rum
Juice 1 lime

3 dashes gum syrup

Shake well with cracked ice and strain.

Wedding Breakfast Cocktail

This is indeed a fine thing to help a person remember his honey-moon.

1 jigger sherry
1 fresh egg
1 tsp. powdered sugar

1 drop Tabasco sauce *or*
sprinkle cayenne

Shake up well without ice and strain into glass.

TERMS USED IN PREPARING FOOD

Adobado—Thin sheets of pork or beef, marinated in vinegar, seasoned, and dried.

Adobar—To marinate, season and rub dry meat, especially pork.

Adobo—Seasonings that are rubbed on meat before drying or cooking.

Al horno—Baked or roasted in the oven. The roasting or baking is always done without a cover.

Asado—Meat roasted on top of the heat in a covered container.

Asar—To roast something quickly, generally over an open flame; used particularly with chiles, onions, and tomatoes.

Chamuscar—Sear, singe or scorch.

Cocer—To cook; however it is used only to cook something in water.

Colar—To strain, sieve or filter.

Confeccionar—To prepare food; not as common as *guisar*.

Cuajar—To coagulate or curdle.

Deshebrar—To shred or ravel into threads.

Desleír—Dissolve anything or thin it in liquid.

Empanizar—Dampen in beaten eggs and milk and dip in crumbs.

Enharinar—To roll in flour for frying.

Enjuagar—To rinse.

En nogada—With nuts.

En parrilla—Grilled.

Escabeche—A pickling marinade.

Espesar—To thicken or coagulate.

Estilar—To drain as of oil or water.

Estofado—A meat and vegetable stew.

Estofar—To stew.

Freír—To fry.

Frito—Fried. e.g. *huevos fritos*—fried eggs.

Gratinar—Cover food with cheese, butter or bread crumbs and brown.

Guisado—Meat and vegetables prepared separately and served on a platter unmixed; similar to a pot roast or stew.

Guisar—To prepare any dish; the word is used as we use "to cook."

Lamprear—To dress or season with wine or sour gravy.

Machacar—To pound or crush.

Macerar—Marinate or soak in wine or vinegar; to mash.

Mechar—To wrap meat in bacon or ham.

179

Menear—To stir or shake.

Moler—To grind.

Picar—To chop, mince or hash.

Rallar—To grate.

Rebanar—To slice.

Rebozar—To bathe food in beaten eggs and fry.

Recalentar—To reheat a food. Certain Mexican foods are cooled then reheated before serving for the first time.

Reducir—To cook until liquid is reduced.

Refreír—To refry. e.g. *frijoles refritos*—refried beans.

Rellenar—To stuff e.g. *chiles rellenos*—stuffed peppers.

Remover—To stir by rocking or shaking.

Requemar—To parch or overcook.

Retazar—Tear into pieces or shred.

Saltear—To fry anything rapidly with no liquid and move it rapidly so it doesn't burn.

Sancochar—To boil food in salted water; *cocer* is used the same way.

Sofreír—To fry lightly.

Tatemar—To cook food in the ground; little used except in a special dish called *tatemado*—which isn't pit cooked.

Trabajar—To beat a sauce or *masa* until it is smooth.

Untar—To oil or butter anything.

Vertir—Beat or whip in.

aceite—oil
aceituna—olive
ajo—garlic
alcachofa—artichoke
alcaparra—caper
apio—celery
arroz—rice
atún—tuna fish
azafrán—saffron
bacalao—cod fish
berenjena—egg plant
betabel—red beet; also called *remolacha*
bolillo—hard rolls
calabaza—any type of squash or gourd
caldo—broth or liquid soup; *sopa* may be liquid or dry soup
camarón—shrimp
canela—cinnamon
cangrejo—crab; generally called *jaiba* in Mexico
carne—meat
carne de res—beef
carnero—mutton
castañas—chestunts
cebolla—onion
cerdo—pork; should be *carne de cerdo,* but *cerdo* or *puerco* are used
   interchangeably
champiñón, champignon—small mushroom
chícharo—pea
chorizo—Mexican pork sausage
chuleta de cerdo—pork chop
cilantro—coriander
clavo de especie—clove
col—cabbage; also *repollo*
comino—cumin
costillas—ribs, chops
durazno—peach
ejote—green beans
elote—green corn
epazote—herb used in cooking—*chenopodium ambrosioides L*

espárrago—asparagus
fresa—strawberry
fideos—vermicelli
frijoles—beans
fruta en vinagre—carrots, chilis, onions, potatoes and other vegetables pickled in vinegar. (three days)
ganso—goose
garbanzo—chick pea
gengibre—ginger
guachinango—red snapper; possibly Mexico's most popular fish
guajolote—turkey; the Spanish name is *pavo*
harina—flour
hierbas de olor—leaf each of bay, thyme, marjoram and oregano
hígado—liver
hongo—large mushroom; or *champiñon*—small ones
huevos—eggs
jaiba—crab; Spanish name is *cangrejo*
jamón—ham
jarabe—syrup; *miel,* honey, is frequently used for syrup
jocoque—cottage cheese
jugo—juice
jugo de naranja—orange juice
langosta—lobster
laurel—bay leaves
leche—milk
lechuga—lettuce
lengua—tongue
lenteja—lentils
levadura—yeast, ferment
limón—lime in Latin America. lemon in Spain. The lemon seen in Mexico is generally sweet.
longaniza—choice pork sausage
maicena—corn starch
manteca—lard
mantequilla—butter
manzana—apple
membrillo—quince
mermelada—marmalade or jam
miel—honey, frequently used to mean syrup
mortadela—bologna
mostaza—mustard

nabo—turnip

naranja—orange

nuez—nut, sp. walnut

nuez moscada—nutmeg

orégano—oregano, wild marjoram, a herb widely used in Mexican cookery

ostión—oyster

paloma—dove

pan—bread; *pan blanco*, white bread, generally means rolls

papa, patata—potato

pasa—raisin

pato—duck

pechuga—breast of chicken. Also choice *tequila*

pepino—cucumber

perejil—parsley

pescado—fish that has been caught; it's a *pez* as long as it swims.

pez sierra—Spanish mackerel

pimienta—black pepper

pollo—chicken

porro—leek

queso—cheese; *queso añejo*—aged cheese

rábano—radish

recaudo—sauce of onion and tomato used in cooking

remolacha—red beet; also *betabel* and *betarraga* in Spain

repollo—cabbage; *col* is more common

riñones—kidneys

robalo—snook; excellent fish popular on both coasts

sal—salt

salsa—sauce. *Salsa picante*—hot sauce. *Salsa mexicana*—fresh sauce made of tomatoes, onion, green chili and coriander

sandía—watermelon

tallarín—noodle

tocino—bacon

ternero—veal

tomate or *jitomate*—tomato

tomillo—thyme

trucha—trout

venado—deer

verdolaga—purslane. Used as a potherb or in salads in parts of the U. S.; it is a must with pork dishes in Mexico.

zanahoria—carrot

CONVERSION TABLES FOR FOREIGN EQUIVALENTS

DRY INGREDIENTS

Ounces	Grams	Grams	Ounces	Pounds	Kilograms	Kilograms	Pounds
1 =	28.35	1 =	0.035	1 =	0.454	1 =	2.205
2	56.70	2	0.07	2	0.91	2	4.41
3	85.05	3	0.11	3	1.36	3	6.61
4	113.40	4	0.14	4	1.81	4	8.82
5	141.75	5	0.18	5	2.27	5	11.02
6	170.10	6	0.21	6	2.72	6	13.23
7	198.45	7	0.25	7	3.18	7	15.43
8	226.80	8	0.28	8	3.63	8	17.64
9	255.15	9	0.32	9	4.08	9	19.84
10	283.50	10	0.35	10	4.54	10	22.05
11	311.85	11	0.39	11	4.99	11	24.26
12	340.20	12	0.42	12	5.44	12	26.46
13	368.55	13	0.46	13	5.90	13	28.67
14	396.90	14	0.49	14	6.35	14	30.87
15	425.25	15	0.53	15	6.81	15	33.08
16	453.60	16	0.57				

LIQUID INGREDIENTS

Liquid Ounces	Milliliters	Milliliters	Liquid Ounces	Quarts	Liters	Liters	Quarts
1 =	29.573	1 =	0.034	1 =	0.946	1 =	1.057
2	59.15	2	0.07	2	1.89	2	2.11
3	88.72	3	0.10	3	2.84	3	3.17
4	118.30	4	0.14	4	3.79	4	4.23
5	147.87	5	0.17	5	4.73	5	5.28
6	177.44	6	0.20	6	5.68	6	6.34
7	207.02	7	0.24	7	6.62	7	7.40
8	236.59	8	0.27	8	7.57	8	8.45
9	266.16	9	0.30	9	8.52	9	9.51
10	295.73	10	0.33	10	9.47	10	10.57

Gallons (American)	Liters	Liters	Gallons (American)
1 =	3.785	1 =	0.264
2	7.57	2	0.53
3	11.36	3	0.79
4	15.14	4	1.06
5	18.93	5	1.32
6	22.71	6	1.59
7	26.50	7	1.85
8	30.28	8	2.11
9	34.07	9	2.38
10	37.86	10	2.74

Index

(SPANISH)

Index

(ENGLISH)

A CATALOG OF
SELECTED DOVER BOOKS
IN ALL FIELDS OF INTEREST

A CATALOG OF SELECTED DOVER
BOOKS IN ALL FIELDS OF INTEREST

CONCERNING THE SPIRITUAL IN ART, Wassily Kandinsky. Pioneering work by father of abstract art. Thoughts on color theory, nature of art. Analysis of earlier masters. 12 illustrations. 80pp. of text. 5⅜ × 8½.   23411-8 Pa. $2.50

LEONARDO ON THE HUMAN BODY, Leonardo da Vinci. More than 1200 of Leonardo's anatomical drawings on 215 plates. Leonardo's text, which accompanies the drawings, has been translated into English. 506pp. 8⅜ × 11¾.
24483-0 Pa. $10.95

GOBLIN MARKET, Christina Rossetti. Best-known work by poet comparable to Emily Dickinson, Alfred Tennyson. With 46 delightfully grotesque illustrations by Laurence Housman. 64pp. 4 × 6¾.   24516-0 Pa. $2.50

THE HEART OF THOREAU'S JOURNALS, edited by Odell Shepard. Selections from *Journal*, ranging over full gamut of interests. 228pp. 5⅜ × 8½.
20741-2 Pa. $4.50

MR. LINCOLN'S CAMERA MAN: MATHEW B. BRADY, Roy Meredith. Over 300 Brady photos reproduced directly from original negatives, photos. Lively commentary. 368pp. 8⅜ × 11¼.   23021-X Pa. $11.95

PHOTOGRAPHIC VIEWS OF SHERMAN'S CAMPAIGN, George N. Barnard. Reprint of landmark 1866 volume with 61 plates: battlefield of New Hope Church, the Etawah Bridge, the capture of Atlanta, etc. 80pp. 9 × 12.   23445-2 Pa. $6.00

A SHORT HISTORY OF ANATOMY AND PHYSIOLOGY FROM THE GREEKS TO HARVEY, Dr. Charles Singer. Thoroughly engrossing non-technical survey. 270 illustrations. 211pp. 5⅜ × 8½.   20389-1 Pa. $4.50

REDOUTE ROSES IRON-ON TRANSFER PATTERNS, Barbara Christopher. Redouté was botanical painter to the Empress Josephine; transfer his famous roses onto fabric with these 24 transfer patterns. 80pp. 8¼ × 10⅞.   24292-7 Pa. $3.50

THE FIVE BOOKS OF ARCHITECTURE, Sebastiano Serlio. Architectural milestone, first (1611) English translation of Renaissance classic. Unabridged reproduction of original edition includes over 300 woodcut illustrations. 416pp. 9⅜ × 12¼.   24349-4 Pa. $14.95

CARLSON'S GUIDE TO LANDSCAPE PAINTING, John F. Carlson. Authoritative, comprehensive guide covers, every aspect of landscape painting. 34 reproductions of paintings by author; 58 explanatory diagrams. 144pp. 8⅜ × 11.
22927-0 Pa. $4.95

101 PUZZLES IN THOUGHT AND LOGIC, C.R. Wylie, Jr. Solve murders, robberies, see which fishermen are liars—purely by reasoning! 107pp. 5⅜ × 8½.
20367-0 Pa. $2.00

TEST YOUR LOGIC, George J. Summers. 50 more truly new puzzles with new turns of thought, new subtleties of inference. 100pp. 5⅜ × 8½.   22877-0 Pa. $2.25

THE MURDER BOOK OF J.G. REEDER, Edgar Wallace. Eight suspenseful stories by bestselling mystery writer of 20s and 30s. Features the donnish Mr. J.G. Reeder of Public Prosecutor's Office. 128pp. 5⅜ × 8½. (Available in U.S. only)
24374-5 Pa. $3.50

ANNE ORR'S CHARTED DESIGNS, Anne Orr. Best designs by premier needlework designer, all on charts: flowers, borders, birds, children, alphabets, etc. Over 100 charts, 10 in color. Total of 40pp. 8¼ × 11.   23704-4 Pa. $2.25

BASIC CONSTRUCTION TECHNIQUES FOR HOUSES AND SMALL BUILDINGS SIMPLY EXPLAINED, U.S. Bureau of Naval Personnel. Grading, masonry, woodworking, floor and wall framing, roof framing, plastering, tile setting, much more. Over 675 illustrations. 568pp. 6½ × 9¼.   20242-9 Pa. $8.95

MATISSE LINE DRAWINGS AND PRINTS, Henri Matisse. Representative collection of female nudes, faces, still lifes, experimental works, etc., from 1898 to 1948. 50 illustrations. 48pp. 8⅜ × 11¼.   23877-6 Pa. $2.50

HOW TO PLAY THE CHESS OPENINGS, Eugene Znosko-Borovsky. Clear, profound examinations of just what each opening is intended to do and how opponent can counter. Many sample games. 147pp. 5⅜ × 8½.   22795-2 Pa. $2.95

DUPLICATE BRIDGE, Alfred Sheinwold. Clear, thorough, easily followed account: rules, etiquette, scoring, strategy, bidding; Goren's point-count system, Blackwood and Gerber conventions, etc. 158pp. 5⅜ × 8½.   22741-3 Pa. $3.00

SARGENT PORTRAIT DRAWINGS, J.S. Sargent. Collection of 42 portraits reveals technical skill and intuitive eye of noted American portrait painter, John Singer Sargent. 48pp. 8¼ × 11⅛.   24524-1 Pa. $2.95

ENTERTAINING SCIENCE EXPERIMENTS WITH EVERYDAY OBJECTS, Martin Gardner. Over 100 experiments for youngsters. Will amuse, astonish, teach, and entertain. Over 100 illustrations. 127pp. 5⅜ × 8½.   24201-3 Pa. $2.50

TEDDY BEAR PAPER DOLLS IN FULL COLOR: A Family of Four Bears and Their Costumes, Crystal Collins. A family of four Teddy Bear paper dolls and nearly 60 cut-out costumes. Full color, printed one side only. 32pp. 9¼ × 12¼.
24550-0 Pa. $3.50

NEW CALLIGRAPHIC ORNAMENTS AND FLOURISHES, Arthur Baker. Unusual, multi-useable material: arrows, pointing hands, brackets and frames, ovals, swirls, birds, etc. Nearly 700 illustrations. 80pp. 8⅜ × 11¼.
24095-9 Pa. $3.75

DINOSAUR DIORAMAS TO CUT & ASSEMBLE, M. Kalmenoff. Two complete three-dimensional scenes in full color, with 31 cut-out animals and plants. Excellent educational toy for youngsters. Instructions; 2 assembly diagrams. 32pp. 9¼ × 12¼.   24541-1 Pa. $3.95

SILHOUETTES: A PICTORIAL ARCHIVE OF VARIED ILLUSTRATIONS, edited by Carol Belanger Grafton. Over 600 silhouettes from the 18th to 20th centuries. Profiles and full figures of men, women, children, birds, animals, groups and scenes, nature, ships, an alphabet. 144pp. 8⅜ × 11¼.   23781-8 Pa. $4.95

25 KITES THAT FLY, Leslie Hunt. Full, easy-to-follow instructions for kites made from inexpensive materials. Many novelties. 70 illustrations. 110pp. 5⅜ × 8½.
22550-X Pa. $2.25

PIANO TUNING, J. Cree Fischer. Clearest, best book for beginner, amateur. Simple repairs, raising dropped notes, tuning by easy method of flattened fifths. No previous skills needed. 4 illustrations. 201pp. 5⅜ × 8½. 23267-0 Pa. $3.50

EARLY AMERICAN IRON-ON TRANSFER PATTERNS, edited by Rita Weiss. 75 designs, borders, alphabets, from traditional American sources. 48pp. 8¼ × 11.
23162-3 Pa. $1.95

CROCHETING EDGINGS, edited by Rita Weiss. Over 100 of the best designs for these lovely trims for a host of household items. Complete instructions, illustrations. 48pp. 8¼ × 11. 24031-2 Pa. $2.25

FINGER PLAYS FOR NURSERY AND KINDERGARTEN, Emilie Poulsson. 18 finger plays with music (voice and piano); entertaining, instructive. Counting, nature lore, etc. Victorian classic. 53 illustrations. 80pp. 6½ × 9¼. 22588-7 Pa. $1.95

BOSTON THEN AND NOW, Peter Vanderwarker. Here in 59 side-by-side views are photographic documentations of the city's past and present. 119 photographs. Full captions. 122pp. 8¼ × 11. 24312-5 Pa. $6.95

CROCHETING BEDSPREADS, edited by Rita Weiss. 22 patterns, originally published in three instruction books 1939-41. 39 photos, 8 charts. Instructions. 48pp. 8¼ × 11. 23610-2 Pa. $2.00

HAWTHORNE ON PAINTING, Charles W. Hawthorne. Collected from notes taken by students at famous Cape Cod School; hundreds of direct, personal *apercus*, ideas, suggestions. 91pp. 5⅜ × 8½. 20653-X Pa. $2.50

THERMODYNAMICS, Enrico Fermi. A classic of modern science. Clear, organized treatment of systems, first and second laws, entropy, thermodynamic potentials, etc. Calculus required. 160pp. 5⅜ × 8½. 60361-X Pa. $4.00

TEN BOOKS ON ARCHITECTURE, Vitruvius. The most important book ever written on architecture. Early Roman aesthetics, technology, classical orders, site selection, all other aspects. Morgan translation. 331pp. 5⅜ × 8½. 20645-9 Pa. $5.50

THE CORNELL BREAD BOOK, Clive M. McCay and Jeanette B. McCay. Famed high-protein recipe incorporated into breads, rolls, buns, coffee cakes, pizza, pie crusts, more. Nearly 50 illustrations. 48pp. 8¼ × 11. 23995-0 Pa. $2.00

THE CRAFTSMAN'S HANDBOOK, Cennino Cennini. 15th-century handbook, school of Giotto, explains applying gold, silver leaf; gesso; fresco painting, grinding pigments, etc. 142pp. 6⅛ × 9¼. 20054-X Pa. $3.50

FRANK LLOYD WRIGHT'S FALLINGWATER, Donald Hoffmann. Full story of Wright's masterwork at Bear Run, Pa. 100 photographs of site, construction, and details of completed structure. 112pp. 9¼ × 10. 23671-4 Pa. $6.50

OVAL STAINED GLASS PATTERN BOOK, C. Eaton. 60 new designs framed in shape of an oval. Greater complexity, challenge with sinuous cats, birds, mandalas framed in antique shape. 64pp. 8¼ × 11. 24519-5 Pa. $3.50

THE BOOK OF WOOD CARVING, Charles Marshall Sayers. Still finest book for beginning student. Fundamentals, technique; gives 34 designs, over 34 projects for panels, bookends, mirrors, etc. 33 photos. 118pp. 7¾ × 10⅝. 23654-4 Pa. $3.95

CARVING COUNTRY CHARACTERS, Bill Higginbotham. Expert advice for beginning, advanced carvers on materials, techniques for creating 18 projects—mirthful panorama of American characters. 105 illustrations. 80pp. 8⅜ × 11. 24135-1 Pa. $2.50

300 ART NOUVEAU DESIGNS AND MOTIFS IN FULL COLOR, C.B. Grafton. 44 full-page plates display swirling lines and muted colors typical of Art Nouveau. Borders, frames, panels, cartouches, dingbats, etc. 48pp. 9⅜ × 12¼. 24354-0 Pa. $6.00

SELF-WORKING CARD TRICKS, Karl Fulves. Editor of *Pallbearer* offers 72 tricks that work automatically through nature of card deck. No sleight of hand needed. Often spectacular. 42 illustrations. 113pp. 5⅜ × 8½. 23334-0 Pa. $3.50

CUT AND ASSEMBLE A WESTERN FRONTIER TOWN, Edmund V. Gillon, Jr. Ten authentic full-color buildings on heavy cardboard stock in H-O scale. Sheriff's Office and Jail, Saloon, Wells Fargo, Opera House, others. 48pp. 9¼ × 12¼. 23736-2 Pa. $3.95

CUT AND ASSEMBLE AN EARLY NEW ENGLAND VILLAGE, Edmund V. Gillon, Jr. Printed in full color on heavy cardboard stock. 12 authentic buildings in H-O scale: Adams home in Quincy, Mass., Oliver Wight house in Sturbridge, smithy, store, church, others. 48pp. 9¼ × 12¼. 23536-X Pa. $3.95

THE TALE OF TWO BAD MICE, Beatrix Potter. Tom Thumb and Hunca Munca squeeze out of their hole and go exploring. 27 full-color Potter illustrations. 59pp. 4¼ × 5½. (Available in U.S. only) 23065-1 Pa. $1.50

CARVING FIGURE CARICATURES IN THE OZARK STYLE, Harold L. Enlow. Instructions and illustrations for ten delightful projects, plus general carving instructions. 22 drawings and 47 photographs altogether. 39pp. 8⅜ × 11. 23151-8 Pa. $2.50

A TREASURY OF FLOWER DESIGNS FOR ARTISTS, EMBROIDERERS AND CRAFTSMEN, Susan Gaber. 100 garden favorites lushly rendered by artist for artists, craftsmen, needleworkers. Many form frames, borders. 80pp. 8¼ × 11. 24096-7 Pa. $3.50

CUT & ASSEMBLE A TOY THEATER/THE NUTCRACKER BALLET, Tom Tierney. Model of a complete, full-color production of Tchaikovsky's classic. 6 backdrops, dozens of characters, familiar dance sequences. 32pp. 9⅜ × 12¼. 24194-7 Pa. $4.50

ANIMALS: 1,419 COPYRIGHT-FREE ILLUSTRATIONS OF MAMMALS, BIRDS, FISH, INSECTS, ETC., edited by Jim Harter. Clear wood engravings present, in extremely lifelike poses, over 1,000 species of animals. 284pp. 9 × 12. 23766-4 Pa. $9.95

MORE HAND SHADOWS, Henry Bursill. For those at their 'finger ends," 16 more effects—Shakespeare, a hare, a squirrel, Mr. Punch, and twelve more—each explained by a full-page illustration. Considerable period charm. 30pp. 6½ × 9¼. 21384-6 Pa. $1.95

SURREAL STICKERS AND UNREAL STAMPS, William Rowe. 224 haunting, hilarious stamps on gummed, perforated stock, with images of elephants, geisha girls, George Washington, etc. 16pp. one side. 8¼ × 11.   24371-0 Pa. $3.50

GOURMET KITCHEN LABELS, Ed Sibbett, Jr. 112 full-color labels (4 copies each of 28 designs). Fruit, bread, other culinary motifs. Gummed and perforated. 16pp. 8¼ × 11.   24087-8 Pa. $2.95

PATTERNS AND INSTRUCTIONS FOR CARVING AUTHENTIC BIRDS, H.D. Green. Detailed instructions, 27 diagrams, 85 photographs for carving 15 species of birds so life-like, they'll seem ready to fly! 8¼ × 11.   24222-6 Pa. $2.75

FLATLAND, E.A. Abbott. Science-fiction classic explores life of 2-D being in 3-D world. 16 illustrations. 103pp. 5⅜ × 8.   20001-9 Pa. $2.00

DRIED FLOWERS, Sarah Whitlock and Martha Rankin. Concise, clear, practical guide to dehydration, glycerinizing, pressing plant material, and more. Covers use of silica gel. 12 drawings. 32pp. 5⅜ × 8½.   21802-3 Pa. $1.00

EASY-TO-MAKE CANDLES, Gary V. Guy. Learn how easy it is to make all kinds of decorative candles. Step-by-step instructions. 82 illustrations. 48pp. 8¼ × 11.
23881-4 Pa. $2.50

SUPER STICKERS FOR KIDS, Carolyn Bracken. 128 gummed and perforated full-color stickers: GIRL WANTED, KEEP OUT, BORED OF EDUCATION, X-RATED, COMBAT ZONE, many others. 16pp. 8¼ × 11.   24092-4 Pa. $2.50

CUT AND COLOR PAPER MASKS, Michael Grater. Clowns, animals, funny faces...simply color them in, cut them out, and put them together, and you have 9 paper masks to play with and enjoy. 32pp. 8¼ × 11.   23171-2 Pa. $2.25

A CHRISTMAS CAROL: THE ORIGINAL MANUSCRIPT, Charles Dickens. Clear facsimile of Dickens manuscript, on facing pages with final printed text. 8 illustrations by John Leech, 4 in color on covers. 144pp. 8⅜ × 11¼.
20980-6 Pa. $5.95

CARVING SHOREBIRDS, Harry V. Shourds & Anthony Hillman. 16 full-size patterns (all double-page spreads) for 19 North American shorebirds with step-by-step instructions. 72pp. 9¼ × 12¼.   24287-0 Pa. $4.95

THE GENTLE ART OF MATHEMATICS, Dan Pedoe. Mathematical games, probability, the question of infinity, topology, how the laws of algebra work, problems of irrational numbers, and more. 42 figures. 143pp. 5⅜ × 8½. (EBE)
22949-1 Pa. $3.50

READY-TO-USE DOLLHOUSE WALLPAPER, Katzenbach & Warren, Inc. Stripe, 2 floral stripes, 2 allover florals, polka dot; all in full color. 4 sheets (350 sq. in.) of each, enough for average room. 48pp. 8¼ × 11.   23495-9 Pa. $2.95

MINIATURE IRON-ON TRANSFER PATTERNS FOR DOLLHOUSES, DOLLS, AND SMALL PROJECTS, Rita Weiss and Frank Fontana. Over 100 miniature patterns: rugs, bedspreads, quilts, chair seats, etc. In standard dollhouse size. 48pp. 8¼ × 11.   23741-9 Pa. $1.95

THE DINOSAUR COLORING BOOK, Anthony Rao. 45 renderings of dinosaurs, fossil birds, turtles, other creatures of Mesozoic Era. Scientifically accurate. Captions. 48pp. 8¼ × 11.   24022-3 Pa. $2.25

JAPANESE DESIGN MOTIFS, Matsuya Co. Mon, or heraldic designs. Over 4000 typical, beautiful designs: birds, animals, flowers, swords, fans, geometrics; all beautifully stylized. 213pp. 11⅜ × 8¼.   22874-6 Pa. $7.95

THE TALE OF BENJAMIN BUNNY, Beatrix Potter. Peter Rabbit's cousin coaxes him back into Mr. McGregor's garden for a whole new set of adventures. All 27 full-color illustrations. 59pp. 4¼ × 5½. (Available in U.S. only)   21102-9 Pa. $1.50

THE TALE OF PETER RABBIT AND OTHER FAVORITE STORIES BOXED SET, Beatrix Potter. Seven of Beatrix Potter's best-loved tales including Peter Rabbit in a specially designed, durable boxed set. 4¼ × 5½. Total of 447pp. 158 color illustrations. (Available in U.S. only)   23903-9 Pa. $10.80

PRACTICAL MENTAL MAGIC, Theodore Annemann. Nearly 200 astonishing feats of mental magic revealed in step-by-step detail. Complete advice on staging, patter, etc. Illustrated. 320pp. 5⅜ × 8½.   24426-1 Pa. $5.95

CELEBRATED CASES OF JUDGE DEE (DEE GOONG AN), translated by Robert Van Gulik. Authentic 18th-century Chinese detective novel; Dee and associates solve three interlocked cases. Led to van Gulik's own stories with same characters. Extensive introduction. 9 illustrations. 237pp. 5⅜ × 8½.

23337-5 Pa. $4.50

CUT & FOLD EXTRATERRESTRIAL INVADERS THAT FLY, M. Grater. Stage your own lilliputian space battles.By following the step-by-step instructions and explanatory diagrams you can launch 22 full-color fliers into space. 36pp. 8¼ × 11.   24478-4 Pa. $2.95

CUT & ASSEMBLE VICTORIAN HOUSES, Edmund V. Gillon, Jr. Printed in full color on heavy cardboard stock, 4 authentic Victorian houses in H-O scale: Italian-style Villa, Octagon, Second Empire, Stick Style. 48pp. 9¼ × 12¼.

23849-0 Pa. $3.95

BEST SCIENCE FICTION STORIES OF H.G. WELLS, H.G. Wells. Full novel *The Invisible Man*, plus 17 short stories: "The Crystal Egg," "Aepyornis Island," "The Strange Orchid," etc. 303pp. 5⅜ × 8½. (Available in U.S. only)

21531-8 Pa. $4.95

TRADEMARK DESIGNS OF THE WORLD, Yusaku Kamekura. A lavish collection of nearly 700 trademarks, the work of Wright, Loewy, Klee, Binder, hundreds of others. 160pp. 8¾ × 8. (Available in U.S. only)   24191-2 Pa. $5.00

THE ARTIST'S AND CRAFTSMAN'S GUIDE TO REDUCING, ENLARGING AND TRANSFERRING DESIGNS, Rita Weiss. Discover, reduce, enlarge, transfer designs from any objects to any craft project. 12pp. plus 16 sheets special graph paper. 8¼ × 11.   24142-4 Pa. $3.25

TREASURY OF JAPANESE DESIGNS AND MOTIFS FOR ARTISTS AND CRAFTSMEN, edited by Carol Belanger Grafton. Indispensable collection of 360 traditional Japanese designs and motifs redrawn in clean, crisp black-and-white, copyright-free illustrations. 96pp. 8¼ × 11.   24435-0 Pa. $3.95

CHANCERY CURSIVE STROKE BY STROKE, Arthur Baker. Instructions and illustrations for each stroke of each letter (upper and lower case) and numerals. 54 full-page plates. 64pp. 8¼ × 11. 24278-1 Pa. $2.50

THE ENJOYMENT AND USE OF COLOR, Walter Sargent. Color relationships, values, intensities; complementary colors, illumination, similar topics. Color in nature and art. 7 color plates, 29 illustrations. 274pp. 5⅜ × 8½. 20944-X Pa. $4.50

SCULPTURE PRINCIPLES AND PRACTICE, Louis Slobodkin. Step-by-step approach to clay, plaster, metals, stone; classical and modern. 253 drawings, photos. 255pp. 8⅛ × 11. 22960-2 Pa. $7.50

VICTORIAN FASHION PAPER DOLLS FROM HARPER'S BAZAR, 1867-1898, Theodore Menten. Four female dolls with 28 elegant high fashion costumes, printed in full color. 32pp. 9¼ × 12¼. 23453-3 Pa. $3.50

FLOPSY, MOPSY AND COTTONTAIL: A Little Book of Paper Dolls in Full Color, Susan LaBelle. Three dolls and 21 costumes (7 for each doll) show Peter Rabbit's siblings dressed for holidays, gardening, hiking, etc. Charming borders, captions. 48pp. 4¼ × 5½. 24376-1 Pa. $2.25

NATIONAL LEAGUE BASEBALL CARD CLASSICS, Bert Randolph Sugar. 83 big-leaguers from 1909-69 on facsimile cards. Hubbell, Dean, Spahn, Brock plus advertising, info, no duplications. Perforated, detachable. 16pp. 8¼ × 11.
24308-7 Pa. $2.95

THE LOGICAL APPROACH TO CHESS, Dr. Max Euwe, et al. First-rate text of comprehensive strategy, tactics, theory for the amateur. No gambits to memorize, just a clear, logical approach. 224pp. 5⅜ × 8½. 24353-2 Pa. $4.50

MAGICK IN THEORY AND PRACTICE, Aleister Crowley. The summation of the thought and practice of the century's most famous necromancer, long hard to find. Crowley's best book. 436pp. 5⅜ × 8½. (Available in U.S. only)
23295-6 Pa. $6.50

THE HAUNTED HOTEL, Wilkie Collins. Collins' last great tale; doom and destiny in a Venetian palace. Praised by T.S. Eliot. 127pp. 5⅜ × 8½.
24333-8 Pa. $3.00

ART DECO DISPLAY ALPHABETS, Dan X. Solo. Wide variety of bold yet elegant lettering in handsome Art Deco styles. 100 complete fonts, with numerals, punctuation, more. 104pp. 8⅛ × 11. 24372-9 Pa. $4.00

CALLIGRAPHIC ALPHABETS, Arthur Baker. Nearly 150 complete alphabets by outstanding contemporary. Stimulating ideas; useful source for unique effects. 154 plates. 157pp. 8⅜ × 11¼. 21045-6 Pa. $4.95

ARTHUR BAKER'S HISTORIC CALLIGRAPHIC ALPHABETS, Arthur Baker. From monumental capitals of first-century Rome to humanistic cursive of 16th century, 33 alphabets in fresh interpretations. 88 plates. 96pp. 9 × 12.
24054-1 Pa. $4.50

LETTIE LANE PAPER DOLLS, Sheila Young. Genteel turn-of-the-century family very popular then and now. 24 paper dolls. 16 plates in full color. 32pp. 9¼ × 12¼. 24089-4 Pa. $3.50

KEYBOARD WORKS FOR SOLO INSTRUMENTS, G.F. Handel. 35 neglected works from Handel's vast oeuvre, originally jotted down as improvisations. Includes Eight Great Suites, others. New sequence. 174pp. 9⅜ × 12¼.
24338-9 Pa. $7.50

AMERICAN LEAGUE BASEBALL CARD CLASSICS, Bert Randolph Sugar. 82 stars from 1900s to 60s on facsimile cards. Ruth, Cobb, Mantle, Williams, plus advertising, info, no duplications. Perforated, detachable. 16pp. 8¼ × 11.
24286-2 Pa. $2.95

A TREASURY OF CHARTED DESIGNS FOR NEEDLEWORKERS, Georgia Gorham and Jeanne Warth. 141 charted designs: owl, cat with yarn, tulips, piano, spinning wheel, covered bridge, Victorian house and many others. 48pp. 8¼ × 11.
23558-0 Pa. $1.95

DANISH FLORAL CHARTED DESIGNS, Gerda Bengtsson. Exquisite collection of over 40 different florals: anemone, Iceland poppy, wild fruit, pansies, many others. 45 illustrations. 48pp. 8¼ × 11.
23957-8 Pa. $1.75

OLD PHILADELPHIA IN EARLY PHOTOGRAPHS 1839-1914, Robert F. Looney. 215 photographs: panoramas, street scenes, landmarks, President-elect Lincoln's visit, 1876 Centennial Exposition, much more. 230pp. 8⅞ × 11¾.
23345-6 Pa. $9.95

PRELUDE TO MATHEMATICS, W.W. Sawyer. Noted mathematician's lively, stimulating account of non-Euclidean geometry, matrices, determinants, group theory, other topics. Emphasis on novel, striking aspects. 224pp. 5⅜ × 8½.
24401-6 Pa. $4.50

ADVENTURES WITH A MICROSCOPE, Richard Headstrom. 59 adventures with clothing fibers, protozoa, ferns and lichens, roots and leaves, much more. 142 illustrations. 232pp. 5⅜ × 8½.
23471-1 Pa. $3.95

IDENTIFYING ANIMAL TRACKS: MAMMALS, BIRDS, AND OTHER ANIMALS OF THE EASTERN UNITED STATES, Richard Headstrom. For hunters, naturalists, scouts, nature-lovers. Diagrams of tracks, tips on identification. 128pp. 5⅜ × 8.
24442-3 Pa. $3.50

VICTORIAN FASHIONS AND COSTUMES FROM HARPER'S BAZAR, 1867-1898, edited by Stella Blum. Day costumes, evening wear, sports clothes, shoes, hats, other accessories in over 1,000 detailed engravings. 320pp. 9⅜ × 12¼.
22990-4 Pa. $9.95

EVERYDAY FASHIONS OF THE TWENTIES AS PICTURED IN SEARS AND OTHER CATALOGS, edited by Stella Blum. Actual dress of the Roaring Twenties, with text by Stella Blum. Over 750 illustrations, captions. 156pp. 9 × 12.
24134-3 Pa. $8.50

HALL OF FAME BASEBALL CARDS, edited by Bert Randolph Sugar. Cy Young, Ted Williams, Lou Gehrig, and many other Hall of Fame greats on 92 full-color, detachable reprints of early baseball cards. No duplication of cards with *Classic Baseball Cards.* 16pp. 8¼ × 11. 23624-2 Pa. $3.50

THE ART OF HAND LETTERING, Helm Wotzkow. Course in hand lettering, Roman, Gothic, Italic, Block, Script. Tools, proportions, optical aspects, individual variation. Very quality conscious. Hundreds of specimens. 320pp. 5⅜ × 8½.
21797-3 Pa. $4.95

HOW THE OTHER HALF LIVES, Jacob A. Riis. Journalistic record of filth, degradation, upward drive in New York immigrant slums, shops, around 1900. New edition includes 100 original Riis photos, monuments of early photography. 233pp. 10 × 7⅞. 22012-5 Pa. $7.95

CHINA AND ITS PEOPLE IN EARLY PHOTOGRAPHS, John Thomson. In 200 black-and-white photographs of exceptional quality photographic pioneer Thomson captures the mountains, dwellings, monuments and people of 19th-century China. 272pp. 9⅜ × 12¼. 24393-1 Pa. $12.95

GODEY COSTUME PLATES IN COLOR FOR DECOUPAGE AND FRAMING, edited by Eleanor Hasbrouk Rawlings. 24 full-color engravings depicting 19th-century Parisian haute couture. Printed on one side only. 56pp. 8¼ × 11. 23879-2 Pa. $3.95

ART NOUVEAU STAINED GLASS PATTERN BOOK, Ed Sibbett, Jr. 104 projects using well-known themes of Art Nouveau: swirling forms, florals, peacocks, and sensuous women. 60pp. 8¼ × 11. 23577-7 Pa. $3.50

QUICK AND EASY PATCHWORK ON THE SEWING MACHINE: Susan Aylsworth Murwin and Suzzy Payne. Instructions, diagrams show exactly how to machine sew 12 quilts. 48pp. of templates. 50 figures. 80pp. 8¼ × 11. 23770-2 Pa. $3.50

THE STANDARD BOOK OF QUILT MAKING AND COLLECTING, Marguerite Ickis. Full information, full-sized patterns for making 46 traditional quilts, also 150 other patterns. 483 illustrations. 273pp. 6⅞ × 9⅝. 20582-7 Pa. $5.95

LETTERING AND ALPHABETS, J. Albert Cavanagh. 85 complete alphabets lettered in various styles; instructions for spacing, roughs, brushwork. 121pp. 8¾ × 8. 20053-1 Pa. $3.75

LETTER FORMS: 110 COMPLETE ALPHABETS, Frederick Lambert. 110 sets of capital letters; 16 lower case alphabets; 70 sets of numbers and other symbols. 110pp. 8⅛ × 11. 22872-X Pa. $4.50

ORCHIDS AS HOUSE PLANTS, Rebecca Tyson Northen. Grow cattleyas and many other kinds of orchids—in a window, in a case, or under artificial light. 63 illustrations. 148pp. 5⅜ × 8½. 23261-1 Pa. $2.95

THE MUSHROOM HANDBOOK, Louis C.C. Krieger. Still the best popular handbook. Full descriptions of 259 species, extremely thorough text, poisons, folklore, etc. 32 color plates; 126 other illustrations. 560pp. 5⅜ × 8½. 21861-9 Pa. $8.50

THE DORÉ BIBLE ILLUSTRATIONS, Gustave Doré. All wonderful, detailed plates: Adam and Eve, Flood, Babylon, life of Jesus, etc. Brief King James text with each plate. 241 plates. 241pp. 9 × 12. 23004-X Pa. $8.95

THE BOOK OF KELLS: Selected Plates in Full Color, edited by Blanche Cirker. 32 full-page plates from greatest manuscript-icon of early Middle Ages. Fantastic, mysterious. Publisher's Note. Captions. 32pp. 9¾ × 12¼. 24345-1 Pa. $4.50

THE PERFECT WAGNERITE, George Bernard Shaw. Brilliant criticism of the Ring Cycle, with provocative interpretation of politics, economic theories behind the Ring. 136pp. 5⅜ × 8½. (Available in U.S. only) 21707-8 Pa. $3.00

THE RIME OF THE ANCIENT MARINER, Gustave Doré, S.T. Coleridge. Doré's finest work, 34 plates capture moods, subtleties of poem. Full text. 77pp. 9¼ × 12.   22305-1 Pa. $4.95

SONGS OF INNOCENCE, William Blake. The first and most popular of Blake's famous "Illuminated Books," in a facsimile edition reproducing all 31 brightly colored plates. Additional printed text of each poem. 64pp. 5¼ × 7.
22764-2 Pa. $3.00

AN INTRODUCTION TO INFORMATION THEORY, J.R. Pierce. Second (1980) edition of most impressive non-technical account available. Encoding, entropy, noisy channel, related areas, etc. 320pp. 5⅜ × 8½.   24061-4 Pa. $4.95

THE DIVINE PROPORTION: A STUDY IN MATHEMATICAL BEAUTY, H.E. Huntley. "Divine proportion" or "golden ratio" in poetry, Pascal's triangle, philosophy, psychology, music, mathematical figures, etc. Excellent bridge between science and art. 58 figures. 185pp. 5⅜ × 8½.   22254-3 Pa. $3.95

THE DOVER NEW YORK WALKING GUIDE: From the Battery to Wall Street, Mary J. Shapiro. Superb inexpensive guide to historic buildings and locales in lower Manhattan: Trinity Church, Bowling Green, more. Complete Text; maps. 36 illustrations. 48pp. 3⅞ × 9¼.   24225-0 Pa. $2.50

NEW YORK THEN AND NOW, Edward B. Watson, Edmund V. Gillon, Jr. 83 important Manhattan sites: on facing pages early photographs (1875-1925) and 1976 photos by Gillon. 172 illustrations. 171pp. 9¼ × 10.   23361-8 Pa. $7.95

HISTORIC COSTUME IN PICTURES, Braun & Schneider. Over 1450 costumed figures from dawn of civilization to end of 19th century. English captions. 125 plates. 256pp. 8⅜ × 11¼.   23150-X Pa. $7.50

VICTORIAN AND EDWARDIAN FASHION: A Photographic Survey, Alison Gernsheim. First fashion history completely illustrated by contemporary photographs. Full text plus 235 photos, 1840-1914, in which many celebrities appear. 240pp. 6½ × 9¼.   24205-6 Pa. $6.00

CHARTED CHRISTMAS DESIGNS FOR COUNTED CROSS-STITCH AND OTHER NEEDLECRAFTS, Lindberg Press. Charted designs for 45 beautiful needlecraft projects with many yuletide and wintertime motifs. 48pp. 8¼ × 11.
24356-7 Pa. $1.95

101 FOLK DESIGNS FOR COUNTED CROSS-STITCH AND OTHER NEEDLE-CRAFTS, Carter Houck. 101 authentic charted folk designs in a wide array of lovely representations with many suggestions for effective use. 48pp. 8¼ × 11.
24369-9 Pa. $2.25

FIVE ACRES AND INDEPENDENCE, Maurice G. Kains. Great back-to-the-land classic explains basics of self-sufficient farming. The one book to get. 95 illustrations. 397pp. 5⅜ × 8½.   20974-1 Pa. $4.95

A MODERN HERBAL, Margaret Grieve. Much the fullest, most exact, most useful compilation of herbal material. Gigantic alphabetical encyclopedia, from aconite to zedoary, gives botanical information, medical properties, folklore, economic uses, and much else. Indispensable to serious reader. 161 illustrations. 888pp. 6½ × 9¼. (Available in U.S. only)   22798-7, 22799-5 Pa., Two-vol. set $16.45

DECORATIVE NAPKIN FOLDING FOR BEGINNERS, Lillian Oppenheimer and Natalie Epstein. 22 different napkin folds in the shape of a heart, clown's hat, love knot, etc. 63 drawings. 48pp. 8¼ × 11. 23797-4 Pa. $1.95

DECORATIVE LABELS FOR HOME CANNING, PRESERVING, AND OTHER HOUSEHOLD AND GIFT USES, Theodore Menten. 128 gummed, perforated labels, beautifully printed in 2 colors. 12 versions. Adhere to metal, glass, wood, ceramics. 24pp. 8¼ × 11. 23219-0 Pa. $2.95

EARLY AMERICAN STENCILS ON WALLS AND FURNITURE, Janet Waring. Thorough coverage of 19th-century folk art: techniques, artifacts, surviving specimens. 166 illustrations, 7 in color. 147pp. of text. 7⅞ × 10¾. 21906-2 Pa. $9.95

AMERICAN ANTIQUE WEATHERVANES, A.B. & W.T. Westervelt. Extensively illustrated 1883 catalog exhibiting over 550 copper weathervanes and finials. Excellent primary source by one of the principal manufacturers. 104pp. 6⅛ × 9¼. 24396-6 Pa. $3.95

ART STUDENTS' ANATOMY, Edmond J. Farris. Long favorite in art schools. Basic elements, common positions, actions. Full text, 158 illustrations. 159pp. 5⅜ × 8½. 20744-7 Pa. $3.95

BRIDGMAN'S LIFE DRAWING, George B. Bridgman. More than 500 drawings and text teach you to abstract the body into its major masses. Also specific areas of anatomy. 192pp. 6½ × 9¼. (EA) 22710-3 Pa. $4.50

COMPLETE PRELUDES AND ETUDES FOR SOLO PIANO, Frederic Chopin. All 26 Preludes, all 27 Etudes by greatest composer of piano music. Authoritative Paderewski edition. 224pp. 9 × 12. (Available in U.S. only) 24052-5 Pa. $7.50

PIANO MUSIC 1888-1905, Claude Debussy. Deux Arabesques, Suite Bergamesque, Masques, 1st series of Images, etc. 9 others, in corrected editions. 175pp. 9⅜ × 12¼. (ECE) 22771-5 Pa. $5.95

TEDDY BEAR IRON-ON TRANSFER PATTERNS, Ted Menten. 80 iron-on transfer patterns of male and female Teddys in a wide variety of activities, poses, sizes. 48pp. 8¼ × 11. 24596-9 Pa. $2.25

A PICTURE HISTORY OF THE BROOKLYN BRIDGE, M.J. Shapiro. Profusely illustrated account of greatest engineering achievement of 19th century. 167 rare photos & engravings recall construction, human drama. Extensive, detailed text. 122pp. 8¼ × 11. 24403-2 Pa. $7.95

NEW YORK IN THE THIRTIES, Berenice Abbott. Noted photographer's fascinating study shows new buildings that have become famous and old sights that have disappeared forever. 97 photographs. 97pp. 11⅜ × 10. 22967-X Pa. $6.50

MATHEMATICAL TABLES AND FORMULAS, Robert D. Carmichael and Edwin R. Smith. Logarithms, sines, tangents, trig functions, powers, roots, reciprocals, exponential and hyperbolic functions, formulas and theorems. 269pp. 5⅜ × 8½. 60111-0 Pa. $3.75

HANDBOOK OF MATHEMATICAL FUNCTIONS WITH FORMULAS, GRAPHS, AND MATHEMATICAL TABLES, edited by Milton Abramowitz and Irene A. Stegun. Vast compendium: 29 sets of tables, some to as high as 20 places. 1,046pp. 8 × 10½. 61272-4 Pa. $19.95

REASON IN ART, George Santayana. Renowned philosopher's provocative, seminal treatment of basis of art in instinct and experience. Volume Four of *The Life of Reason*. 230pp. 5⅜ × 8.   24358-3 Pa. $4.50

LANGUAGE, TRUTH AND LOGIC, Alfred J. Ayer. Famous, clear introduction to Vienna, Cambridge schools of Logical Positivism. Role of philosophy, elimination of metaphysics, nature of analysis, etc. 160pp. 5⅜ × 8½. (USCO)
20010-8 Pa. $2.75

BASIC ELECTRONICS, U.S. Bureau of Naval Personnel. Electron tubes, circuits, antennas, AM, FM, and CW transmission and receiving, etc. 560 illustrations. 567pp. 6½ × 9¼.   21076-6 Pa. $8.95

THE ART DECO STYLE, edited by Theodore Menten. Furniture, jewelry, metalwork, ceramics, fabrics, lighting fixtures, interior decors, exteriors, graphics from pure French sources. Over 400 photographs. 183pp. 8⅜ × 11¼.
22824-X Pa. $6.95

THE FOUR BOOKS OF ARCHITECTURE, Andrea Palladio. 16th-century classic covers classical architectural remains, Renaissance revivals, classical orders, etc. 1738 Ware English edition. 216 plates. 110pp. of text. 9½ × 12¾.
21308-0 Pa. $11.50

THE WIT AND HUMOR OF OSCAR WILDE, edited by Alvin Redman. More than 1000 ripostes, paradoxes, wisecracks: Work is the curse of the drinking classes, I can resist everything except temptations, etc. 258pp. 5⅜ × 8½. (USCO)
20602-5 Pa. $3.50

THE DEVIL'S DICTIONARY, Ambrose Bierce. Barbed, bitter, brilliant witticisms in the form of a dictionary. Best, most ferocious satire America has produced. 145pp. 5⅜ × 8½.   20487-1 Pa. $2.50

ERTÉ'S FASHION DESIGNS, Erté. 210 black-and-white inventions from *Harper's Bazar*, 1918-32, plus 8pp. full-color covers. Captions. 88pp. 9 × 12.
24203-X Pa. $6.50

ERTÉ GRAPHICS, Erté. Collection of striking color graphics: *Seasons, Alphabet, Numerals, Aces* and *Precious Stones*. 50 plates, including 4 on covers. 48pp. 9⅜ × 12¼.   23580-7 Pa. $6.95

PAPER FOLDING FOR BEGINNERS, William D. Murray and Francis J. Rigney. Clearest book for making origami sail boats, roosters, frogs that move legs, etc. 40 projects. More than 275 illustrations. 94pp. 5⅜ × 8½.   20713-7 Pa. $2.25

ORIGAMI FOR THE ENTHUSIAST, John Montroll. Fish, ostrich, peacock, squirrel, rhinoceros, Pegasus, 19 other intricate subjects. Instructions. Diagrams. 128pp. 9 × 12.   23799-0 Pa. $4.95

CROCHETING NOVELTY POT HOLDERS, edited by Linda Macho. 64 useful, whimsical pot holders feature kitchen themes, animals, flowers, other novelties. Surprisingly easy to crochet. Complete instructions. 48pp. 8¼ × 11.
24296-X Pa. $1.95

CROCHETING DOILIES, edited by Rita Weiss. Irish Crochet, Jewel, Star Wheel, Vanity Fair and more. Also luncheon and console sets, runners and centerpieces. 51 illustrations. 48pp. 8¼ × 11.   23424-X Pa. $2.00

YUCATAN BEFORE AND AFTER THE CONQUEST, Diego de Landa. Only significant account of Yucatan written in the early post-Conquest era. Translated by William Gates. Over 120 illustrations. 162pp. 5⅜ × 8½.   23622-6 Pa. $3.50

ORNATE PICTORIAL CALLIGRAPHY, E.A. Lupfer. Complete instructions, over 150 examples help you create magnificent "flourishes" from which beautiful animals and objects gracefully emerge. 8⅛ × 11.   21957-7 Pa. $2.95

DOLLY DINGLE PAPER DOLLS, Grace Drayton. Cute chubby children by same artist who did Campbell Kids. Rare plates from 1910s. 30 paper dolls and over 100 outfits reproduced in full color. 32pp. 9¼ × 12¼.   23711-7 Pa. $3.50

CURIOUS GEORGE PAPER DOLLS IN FULL COLOR, H. A. Rey, Kathy Allert. Naughty little monkey-hero of children's books in two doll figures, plus 48 full-color costumes: pirate, Indian chief, fireman, more. 32pp. 9¼ × 12¼.
24386-9 Pa. $3.50

GERMAN: HOW TO SPEAK AND WRITE IT, Joseph Rosenberg. Like *French, How to Speak and Write It.* Very rich modern course, with a wealth of pictorial material. 330 illustrations. 384pp. 5⅜ × 8½. (USUKO)   20271-2 Pa. $4.75

CATS AND KITTENS: 24 Ready-to-Mail Color Photo Postcards, D. Holby. Handsome collection; feline in a variety of adorable poses. Identifications. 12pp. on postcard stock. 8¼ × 11.   24469-5 Pa. $2.95

MARILYN MONROE PAPER DOLLS, Tom Tierney. 31 full-color designs on heavy stock, from *The Asphalt Jungle, Gentlemen Prefer Blondes,* 22 others. 1 doll. 16 plates. 32pp. 9⅜ × 12¼.   23769-9 Pa. $3.50

FUNDAMENTALS OF LAYOUT, F.H. Wills. All phases of layout design discussed and illustrated in 121 illustrations. Indispensable as student's text or handbook for professional. 124pp. 8⅜ × 11.   21279-3 Pa. $4.50

FANTASTIC SUPER STICKERS, Ed Sibbett, Jr. 75 colorful pressure-sensitive stickers. Peel off and place for a touch of pizzazz: clowns, penguins, teddy bears, etc. Full color. 16pp. 8¼ × 11.   24471-7 Pa. $2.95

LABELS FOR ALL OCCASIONS, Ed Sibbett, Jr. 6 labels each of 16 different designs—baroque, art nouveau, art deco, Pennsylvania Dutch, etc.—in full color. 24pp. 8¼ × 11.   23688-9 Pa. $2.95

HOW TO CALCULATE QUICKLY: RAPID METHODS IN BASIC MATHEMATICS, Henry Sticker. Addition, subtraction, multiplication, division, checks, etc. More than 8000 problems, solutions. 185pp. 5 × 7¼.   20295-X Pa. $2.95

THE CAT COLORING BOOK, Karen Baldauski. Handsome, realistic renderings of 40 splendid felines, from American shorthair to exotic types. 44 plates. Captions. 48pp. 8¼ × 11.   24011-8 Pa. $2.25

THE TALE OF PETER RABBIT, Beatrix Potter. The inimitable Peter's terrifying adventure in Mr. McGregor's garden, with all 27 wonderful, full-color Potter illustrations. 55pp. 4¼ × 5½. (Available in U.S. only)   22827-4 Pa. $1.60

BASIC ELECTRICITY, U.S. Bureau of Naval Personnel. Batteries, circuits, conductors, AC and DC, inductance and capacitance, generators, motors, transformers, amplifiers, etc. 349 illustrations. 448pp. 6½ × 9¼.   20973-3 Pa. $7.95

CATALOG OF DOVER BOOKS

SOURCE BOOK OF MEDICAL HISTORY, edited by Logan Clendening, M.D. Original accounts ranging from Ancient Egypt and Greece to discovery of X-rays: Galen, Pasteur, Lavoisier, Harvey, Parkinson, others. 685pp. 5⅜ × 8½.
20621-1 Pa. $10.95

THE ROSE AND THE KEY, J.S. Lefanu. Superb mystery novel from Irish master. Dark doings among an ancient and aristocratic English family. Well-drawn characters; capital suspense. Introduction by N. Donaldson. 448pp. 5⅜ × 8½.
24377-X Pa. $6.95

SOUTH WIND, Norman Douglas. Witty, elegant novel of ideas set on languorous Meditterranean island of Nepenthe. Elegant prose, glittering epigrams, mordant satire. 1917 masterpiece. 416pp. 5⅜ × 8½. (Available in U.S. only)
24361-3 Pa. $5.95

RUSSELL'S CIVIL WAR PHOTOGRAPHS, Capt. A.J. Russell. 116 rare Civil War Photos: Bull Run, Virginia campaigns, bridges, railroads, Richmond, Lincoln's funeral car. Many never seen before. Captions. 128pp. 9⅜ × 12¼.
24283-8 Pa. $6.95

PHOTOGRAPHS BY MAN RAY: 105 Works, 1920-1934. Nudes, still lifes, landscapes, women's faces, celebrity portraits (Dali, Matisse, Picasso, others), rayographs. Reprinted from rare gravure edition. 128pp. 9⅜ × 12¼. (Available in U.S. only)
23842-3 Pa. $6.95

STAR NAMES: THEIR LORE AND MEANING, Richard H. Allen. Star names, the zodiac, constellations: folklore and literature associated with heavens. The basic book of its field, fascinating reading. 563pp. 5⅜ × 8½.
21079-0 Pa. $7.95

BURNHAM'S CELESTIAL HANDBOOK, Robert Burnham, Jr. Thorough guide to the stars beyond our solar system. Exhaustive treatment. Alphabetical by constellation: Andromeda to Cetus in Vol. 1; Chamaeleon to Orion in Vol. 2; and Pavo to Vulpecula in Vol. 3. Hundreds of illustrations. Index in Vol. 3. 2000pp. 6⅛ × 9¼.
23567-X, 23568-8, 23673-0 Pa. Three-vol. set $36.85

THE ART NOUVEAU STYLE BOOK OF ALPHONSE MUCHA, Alphonse Mucha. All 72 plates from *Documents Decoratifs* in original color. Stunning, essential work of Art Nouveau. 80pp. 9⅜ × 12¼.
24044-4 Pa. $7.95

DESIGNS BY ERTE; FASHION DRAWINGS AND ILLUSTRATIONS FROM "HARPER'S BAZAR," Erte. 310 fabulous line drawings and 14 *Harper's Bazar* covers, 8 in full color. Erte's exotic temptresses with tassels, fur muffs, long trains, coifs, more. 129pp. 9⅜ × 12¼.
23397-9 Pa. $6.95

HISTORY OF STRENGTH OF MATERIALS, Stephen P. Timoshenko. Excellent historical survey of the strength of materials with many references to the theories of elasticity and structure. 245 figures. 452pp. 5⅜ × 8½. 61187-6 Pa. $8.95

Prices subject to change without notice.

Available at your book dealer or write for free catalog to Dept. GI, Dover Publications, Inc., 31 East 2nd St. Mineola, N.Y. 11501. Dover publishes more than 175 books each year on science, elementary and advanced mathematics, biology, music, art, literary history, social sciences and other areas.